Cesar Millan's
SHORT GUIDE TO A
HAPPY DOG

Cesar Millan's
SHORT GUIDE TO A HAPPY DOG

98 Essential Tips and Techniques

NATIONAL GEOGRAPHIC

WASHINGTON, D.C.

Published by the National Geographic Society
1145 17th Street N.W., Washington, D.C. 20036

ISBN: 978-1-4262-1190-4 (hardcover)
ISBN: 978-1-4262-1200-0 (export edition)

CELEBRATING
‹125›
YEARS

The National Geographic Society is one of the world's largest nonprofit scientific and educational organizations. Founded in 1888 to "increase and diffuse geographic knowledge," the Society's mission is to inspire people to care about the planet. It reaches more than 400 million people worldwide each month through its official journal, *National Geographic,* and other magazines; National Geographic Channel; television documentaries; music; radio; films; books; DVDs; maps; exhibitions; live events; school publishing programs; interactive media; and merchandise. National Geographic has funded more than 10,000 scientific research, conservation, and exploration projects and supports an education program promoting geographic literacy.

The techniques presented in this book are for informational purposes only. As each individual situation is unique, you should use proper discretion, in consideration with a professional dog expert, before utilizing the information contained in this book. The author and publisher expressly disclaim responsibility for any adverse effects that may result from the use or application of the information contained in this book.

For more information, visit www.nationalgeographic.com.
National Geographic Society
1145 17th Street N.W.
Washington, D.C. 20036-4688 U.S.A.

For information about special discounts for bulk purchases, please contact National Geographic Books Special Sales: ngspecsales@ngs.org

For rights or permissions inquiries, please contact National Geographic Books Subsidiary Rights: ngbookrights@ngs.org

Interior design by Melissa Farris

Printed in the United States of America
12/CW-CML/1

Contents

I'm dedicating this book to all the fans around the world.
Without their support, I would not be able to give tips to anybody.
So thanks to my fans for their open-mindedness, and, of course,
to their dogs for being with me for the past nine seasons
of Dog Whisperer.

I am also dedicating this book to Jahira Dar and Calvin Millan
for being there for me and traveling around the world with me
so we can continue to help people.
Without you, my pack is not complete.

Thank you.

ACKNOWLEDGMENTS

I want to thank God for giving me such an amazing gift with dogs. I want to thank my team, including the folks at Cesar Millan Inc., the Dog Psychology Center, Cesar's Way, the National Geographic Channel, Lisa Thomas and Hilary Black at National Geographic Books, and Tara King and the Millan Foundation for their steadfast dedication to the mission of dog rescue, rehabilitation, and adoption. Special thanks to Jon Bastian and Bob Aniello for helping me create this book, and to Amy Briggs, who gave up weekends and evenings to edit these words.

While the last nine years have been amazing, I look forward to the future and want to acknowledge the newer members to my team, including the *Leader of the Pack* TV production crew, Steve LeGrice at *Cesar's Way* magazine, and Cheri Lucas, Evo Fisher, and Eric Rovner of William Morris Endeavor. I also want to thank Pomi for extending his ranch so we can shoot an amazing show.

—CESAR MILLAN

I would like to thank Stacy and Ted Milner for originally bringing me into Cesar's world; my CMI, Cesar's Way, and *Dog Whisperer* packs, past and present; Che'Rae Adams and the L.A. Writers Center for their inspiration, support, and friendship; and my pack, Shadow and Sheeba, for always being there and for teaching me to be their leader. Thanks to Bob Aniello and Dave Rogers for their belief and trust. And, of course, I would like to thank Cesar, from whom I've learned so much over the years, and who has given me the opportunity to work in a field I am so passionate about.

—Jon Bastian

I would like to thank my parents—Al and Jean Aniello—for their total dedication to inspiration; my family—Daryle, Nick, and Chris—for putting up with me and allowing me to be who I am, even when it drives them crazy; my two brothers, Ron and Rick, who have always been there and have guided me creatively, morally, and spiritually. And Cesar for teaching me that all things really are possible.

—Bob Aniello

I would like to thank Cesar Millan and his great team for the opportunity to work on this exciting project. Thank you, Bob and Jon, for moving heaven and earth to deliver the text in under what most would call impossible conditions. You guys are a dream team—fast, open to just about anything, and constantly coming up with new ways to make a book better. Thanks to my husband, Crenshaw, and daughter, Diana. Knowing you're there makes everything possible. Thanks to my gray cats (gasp!), Colonel and Nellie, for the purrs and head butts. And thanks to Hoss, Ralph, Max, Bud, and Lucy for being the best dogs anyone could ask for. I'm so lucky to have shared my life with you.

—Amy Briggs

INTRODUCTION

I'm standing on the soft desert sand as the heels of my shoes dig deeper into the porous desert soil. As I settle in, the sand begins to form a mold around my shoes like cement. It's hot, over 105 degrees. I'm uncomfortable, and it's hard to move.

As I gaze out over the border from the United States into Mexico, it suddenly hits me. I realize I have been living in the United States longer than I lived in Mexico. It's been over 22 years since I crossed the border illegally on December 23, 1990, from Tijuana, into San Ysidro, just south of San Diego, California, when I was 20 years old.

The border was very different then. There were fewer walls and fewer border patrollers, and the desert stretched out for what seemed like an eternity back then. Although so much has changed around me, I recognize the same desert and valleys that I wandered in alone for two weeks before making it safely to San Diego. I can still smell the dryness of the air and feel the nakedness of the terrain where I hid among rocks and bushes to avoid capture. Those feelings of aloneness will never go away, and returning has only intensified the memories of that experience. As I look out across that landscape, I ask myself: How did I do it? I had a simple dream back then to come to the United States and become a dog trainer. It was a dream then, and now it's a reality. This trip is completion for me.

It's September 13, 2012, and I have returned to San Ysidro to the very spot where I crossed illegally. Only this time, I am here not as a lonely and frightened immigrant, but having fulfilled my dream. I'm here with a full camera crew, a photographer, and my production manager Allegra Pickett. I didn't arrive on foot, wandering the desert, but in the comfort of an air-conditioned SUV with National Geographic Television, which is shooting a documentary of my life. It's surreal to me and I am humbled, almost embarrassed that a TV network would find my life story so interesting that it wants to share it with others.

As the cameras roll, a crowd of curious onlookers and fans has begun to form a few yards from us. Most of the people seem to know me by name. Some call out in Spanish, "El Encantador de Perros" (translated as "The One Who Enchants Dogs," as *Dog Whisperer* is called in Mexico). During shooting breaks, I walk over to speak with some of them and sign a few autographs. The diversity of the crowd is amazing and reflects the broad fan base for the TV show that airs in over 100 countries. There is a Canadian woman in her mid-60s who says she has watched all 167 episodes of *Dog Whisperer;* a family from Seattle; a gentleman from Argentina who shares that he has used some of my dog psychology in raising his own children; and a young family from London who tells me they attended my "Cesar Millan Live" seminar when I was touring in March 2010.

As I stand at the border listening to these fans, I realize that although I was born and raised in Mexico and then became a U.S.

*Back to where it all began: my 2012 return to the border
near San Ysidro, California*

citizen in 2009, I don't belong to a country defined by borders, territory, or language. I belong to a worldwide community of people who love dogs. This is my pack. I belong with them . . . and with their dogs. And there are over 400 million dogs and over 1 billion people in this global pack who have a dog in their life. My role within this huge community is that of a Pack Leader.

It's a privilege I take very seriously. As a Pack Leader, I am expected to provide protection and direction. Sure, most people come to me because they are seeking answers to their dog problems. For all nine seasons of *Dog Whisperer,* I showed techniques for correcting every type of misbehavior from every breed imaginable, and I encountered just about every human mistake possible in caring for dogs. But my role as Pack Leader is most important to me now. It's so important that I decided to end the *Dog Whisperer* TV show after the ninth season and create a new show, called *Cesar Millan's Leader of the Pack.*

While *Dog Whisperer* was a show about rehabilitation, *Leader of the Pack* is a show about rescue. It's the story of abandonment and getting a second chance. It's the story of rehabilitation and adoption to a compatible family. For many of the dogs on the show, it's their last chance. In my role as Pack Leader, I'm finding new homes for these incredible dogs while giving their new families the right tools to care for them. While there are only a few people in this world who can be Dog Whisperers, everyone can be a Pack Leader.

This new sense of purpose has compelled me to create this book to help people become Pack Leaders in the same way I have. When I stop to think about it, this guide has been 22 years in the making. It combines all my empirical knowledge of dog psychology and training in one simple, easy-to-read volume.

I have learned so much from Junior, my right-hand dog.

I explain the most important aspects of understanding dogs as dogs and not as humans. I recount how thousands of years of evolution and human intervention in genetic breeding have shaped our canine companions. Next, I explore what I call "Natural Dog Laws" and how they affect dogs' behavior and thinking. In Chapter 3, you'll find my Nine Core Principles, which are short and simple intuitive tools to help you raise a healthy, happy, and balanced dog. These principles and techniques are what I have followed with my own pack and in my rehabilitation work. The following chapters all cover important lessons and strategies for finding the right dog, adjusting to life changes, and correcting common misbehaviors. I then break down each problem and offer solutions so the material is easy to follow and reference.

But what's more, I've filled these pages with what I've learned about human behavior from my work with dogs and from my own life experiences. We will talk more about this in the final chapters, where I will share with you inspiring stories—including my own—from people whose lives have been touched and altered forever by a canine companion. For the very first time, I will share with you insights from work I've done with people like personal life coach and star of *The Biggest Loser* TV show, Jillian Michaels. Such people have made profound changes by applying the Natural Dog Laws, the Core Principles, and Pack Leader Techniques I've developed over numerous years of helping animals and people find harmony together.

And, of course, throughout the book, you'll meet the dogs . . . the obsessive ones, the aggressive ones . . . the ones humanized to the point that they became destabilized and their owners— the very people who caused the problem in the first place—had to give them up or isolate them in cages or backyards. I'll share stories of special dogs from my new show, *Cesar Millan's Leader of the Pack*. You'll see how the methods discussed in this book have helped each of these dogs find balance as well as new loving homes with the perfect family.

By the end of my *Short Guide to a Happy Dog*, you will have traveled on a journey with me into the heart and mind of a dog. You'll gain a rich understanding of how a dog's mind works and how our energy affects dogs' behavior, and you'll learn how to be a good Pack Leader to your dog.

And if I do my job right as Pack Leader, you will gain a better understanding of what's unbalanced in your life and hopefully learn how to better fulfill the needs of your own pack.

It is my hope and belief that this book will bring you insights that improve and enrich your relationship with your dog, your family, and your community. Welcome to the pack.

Before you begin reading, it's important to begin with an open mind. I understand that I use words that make people uncomfortable. In my experience, the two most common are *dominance* and *control*. I believe some people feel uneasy with these terms because they are interpreting them in negative ways. I'd like to explain why, to me, they are neutral, possibly even positive, and necessary.

People frequently ask me what I mean when I use these words. Apparently, in English, and in the United States in particular, such words have negative connotations—nobody likes a spouse or boss who is "controlling," and the concept of "dominance" implies completely conquering or overwhelming an enemy.

When I use these words, these aren't the associations I have with them. The word *dominance* comes from the Latin "dominus," which just means "master." To my ears, this word sounds like the Spanish word *maestro,* which simply means "teacher." In English, the word *maestro* frequently refers to an orchestra conductor—and that is a much more pleasant image to associate with the word *dominance,* because a conductor provides one of the two things that a dominant dog in a pack provides: direction.

The second word that is often misunderstood is *control*. When used in this book, I mean the act of starting, changing, and stopping action by others. When teachers tell their students to begin a test or to put their pencils down at the end, that is control. When a traffic cop makes cars detour because of an accident—changing their direction—this is also control. In your relationship with your dog, you, the human, should be the one who determines when things start, change, and stop. If your dog is the one making these decisions, then you, quite simply, are not in control. To be a Pack Leader, you must be in control.

If you are on a walk and your dog starts to pull ahead, take control by changing direction. If your dog is exhibiting a behavior you do not want, stop it. Provide the correction. Before giving your dog something he wants—a walk, food, water, affection—wait until your dog displays the behavior that *you* want in a calm, submissive state. The action a dog desires does not begin until *you* allow it to start, and never when your dog initiates it.

I strongly believe that embracing these words—*control* and *dominance*—is part of becoming a Pack Leader. It's crucial that you get used to them—in the way that I mean them.

Because humans can have strong negative associations with words, the intellectual act of reading a word can trigger an emotional response—sometimes a defensive one—that can get in the way of understanding. While reading this book, I challenge you to pay attention to your emotions and stop at any word that makes you feel uncomfortable. Underline the word, and then think about why that word generated that response.

Try it right now with *control* and *dominance*. What do each of these words mean to you? Do they give you positive or negative feelings? What is it about each word that might do that? For any words that disturb you, try to come up with synonyms that you find more pleasant. For example, many people may find the word *heat* brings up unpleasant emotions, but *warmth* may be more positive—the scorching desert in summer versus a fireplace and loved ones at a winter holiday party.

To dogs, words don't mean anything. They are just tones and inflection of sound. This includes the names we call them. Dogs communicate with energy, and they respond best to us when we are calm and assertive. To reach the calm state, we need first to control our human emotions, especially the ones that lead to weak energy states, like doubt, fear, or anxiety. If particular words are causing these feelings in you, then you need to neutralize the negatives by identifying why they make you feel that way, removing those connotations from the words, and/or replacing them with synonyms that are neutral to you, if necessary.

Knowledge removes fear, and the aim of this book is to bring you plenty of knowledge. Achieving calmness, however, is up to you. If you work with me and read this book with an open mind, then you will learn to reach that state of calmness, and you will instinctively know how to bring your dogs balance.

CHAPTER ONE

The Canine State of Mind

Now that we're beginning our journey toward a happier life with your dog, it's best to start by seeing the world through his eyes—or more likely, smelling the world through his nose. You first have to try to understand and embrace the canine state of mind.

Have you ever wondered what your dog is thinking as he gazes at you? You're giving him commands like "sit," "quiet," or "get off the couch," and if he's a well-balanced dog, he does them, but what's going on in his brain *when* he does them? Wonder no more. A dog's brain is a marvelous thing. It gives him information about the world, tells him what to do with it, and helps him figure out how to please you, his human.

Dogs are motivated to please people. They know instinctually that people are of utmost importance to them, and that they can get almost any need satisfied if they rely on a human. As a result, dogs do what they can to please humans, and their brains are wired for this impulse.

Dogs are wonderfully adaptable, but this drive to please is a double-edged sword. If you want your dog to behave like a needy child, the dog will eventually behave like a needy child, even though his natural instincts tell him not to. On one hand, dogs' desire to please makes them loving pets and dedicated service dogs, but on the other, it can also get them into the most trouble. When dogs try to adapt to human desires that are unnatural for them, they can become unbalanced.

Understanding how your dog's brain functions can not only help you understand your dog, but it can also help you be a better Pack Leader by giving your dog what she needs to be healthy, happy, and balanced.

▶ Your Dog's Brain

The brain of a dog needs large amounts of fuel to function properly. Although the brain in an average dog accounts for less than one-half of one percent of its body weight, it receives over 20 percent of the blood that is pumped out by the heart.

The brain of a dog is responsible for interpreting and acting upon all the information or signals it receives from the dog's various sensory inputs. To think about it simply, a dog's brain is like a superhighway of sensory information. A dog's responses to these signals have been predetermined by the wiring of her genetic makeup. But it doesn't mean that dogs will always react in the same way to the same stimuli.

The anatomy of the dog's brain is similar to that of most other mammals. The cerebrum controls learning, emotions, and behavior. The cerebellum controls the muscles, and the brain stem connects to the peripheral nervous system.

Anatomy of a Dog's Brain

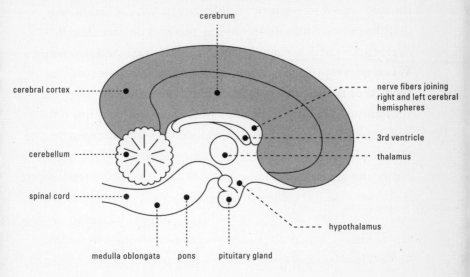

cerebrum

cerebral cortex

nerve fibers joining
right and left cerebral
hemispheres

3rd ventricle

cerebellum

thalamus

spinal cord

hypothalamus

medulla oblongata   pons   pituitary gland

Another network in the brain, called the limbic system, is thought to be the area that controls general memory functions.

A dog understands her own relationship to the world around her through the limbic system, which is fed by her senses — smell, hearing, sight, touch, and taste.

▶ Instincts Versus Training

Sometimes there is a natural conflict between what a dog "instinctively" wants to do and what we want him to do. This tug-of-war plays out in the limbic system of a dog's brain.

Most dog training methods focus on overriding the natural limbic system, either by giving rewards for obeying us and ignoring instincts, or by punishing dogs for following instinctual tendencies.

Most dog training today is focused on these two schools of thought: rewards-based or punishment-based learning. I have used techniques from both training methods in my rehabilitation work, and I always recommend using the methods that are best for you and your dog. Rather than follow one specific method or formula, I always try to tailor my approach based on the unique dog in front of me.

Training is about applying technique. I teach classes at the Dog Psychology Center (DPC) that cover most of the techniques dog trainers commonly use today, such as clicker training and reward-based training. People often insist I don't use clicker techniques in my training, but the "Tsch!" sound I make with my mouth during my rehabilitation sessions is the same as using a clicker. It associates a sound with a particular behavior I want the dog to do. Likewise, I have also used treats to coax fearful dogs into a relaxed state before I begin a rehabilitation session.

During training classes at the Dog Psychology Center, I often hear trainers discussing and even arguing among themselves about which technique is best for a specific situation. When asked for my opinion, I always return to the basics: Know what your particular dog needs; direct the dog's tendencies into healthy activities; and project clear and consistent leadership.

It doesn't matter if you use a treat, a clicker, or discipline to elicit the behavior you want, as long as that behavior is natural.

▶ Work With Instincts, Not Against Them

So many dog problems today occur because humans suppress the natural functioning of the limbic system in dogs. The key to successful dog training is to rechannel a dog's natural energy and instincts to behavior that is positive for both the human and the dog. Redirection instead of suppression is one of my cardinal rules. I always try to nurture and cultivate all the special skills of a specific breed and redirect dogs' natural tendencies into healthy activities.

For example, I receive lots of calls from schnauzer owners complaining that their dog is digging excessively in their backyard. Schnauzers got their name from the word *schnauze*, German for snout. They were bred to hunt for rats and other vermin in barns and homes, and they have a very powerful sense of smell. This breed is only doing what it is instinctually engineered to do. Rather than fight the dog's natural instincts, why not try creating a space where it's acceptable for the dog to dig? Digging is a form of exercise and works off excess energy. The ability to work with the dog's natural instincts may be an easier solution.

At the DPC, we have special areas where dogs can exercise their natural instincts. We have a swimming pool for water dogs and retrievers. We also have a sheepherding area for breeds that have the genetics for herding.

I remember one dog named Ginger that a local rescue organization brought to the DPC. Ginger was so tense and excitable that her owner just gave up on her. I could tell that Ginger was anxiety ridden, and in her current state of mind, Ginger would never be adopted. However, I took Ginger to the sheepherding area, where I don't think I have ever seen a faster transformation. Ginger was herding the sheep in ten minutes, and with her instinctual needs satisfied, she relaxed into a calm, submissive state. We still use Ginger as a TV personality at the Dog Psychology Center whenever we need to demonstrate sheepherding. Ginger can herd sheep faster than any dog I know.

According to Janna Duncan, who teaches our sheepherding classes at the DPC, "Herding is instinctual for a lot of breeds. When they're 'working,' they feel like they have a purpose in life. Letting them work helps with self-confidence and relieves anxiety and aggression." In one class, I watched as Janna introduced a five-month-old puppy to the sheep. Janna let the puppy "find her instincts." Within minutes, the little puppy, named Luna, was instinctively trying to keep the sheep together and get them moving. After the demonstration, Luna proudly walked back to her family and sat quietly and obediently at their feet. Her job was done!

▶ Suppression of Herding Dogs' Instincts

- **Instinctual Tendency** = herding
- **Energy State** = anxiety ridden, unstable
- **Behavior Problem** = tendency to herd other pets or even humans in the home; constant nipping at heels and jumping up on people
- **Solution** = redirect energy into flyball, Frisbee, or agility training
- **Breeds Most Affected** = corgis, shepherds, Belgian Malinois, border collies, briards, German shepherds, sheepdogs, Swedish vallhunds

In certain cases, you may want to do the opposite of nurturing a breed-specific trait. With certain powerful breeds like rottweilers and pit bulls, you may not want to nurture the specific activity that the dog was originally genetically engineered to perform, like hunting or guarding. You'll need to find creative ways to redirect these tendencies. For example, Junior and I love to play tug-of-war. Junior's instinct draws him to hunting. When we play tug-of-war, I rechannel the energy to a game of control.

Repression of natural, instinctual tendencies can lead to serious behavior problems. Ginger is just one example of a dog with a behavior problem that develops when humans override the limbic system. For a variety of reasons, some owners are not able to let their herding dogs herd, their water dogs swim, or their digging dogs dig. In these cases, it's best to accept that these dogs will have excess energy that will need to be drained. Increasing a dog's exercise can burn off that energy, engage the senses, and decrease the unwanted behavior.

▶ What a Dog Remembers

Now that you have a basic understanding of how a dog's brain works and how a dog processes sensory inputs, it's equally important to understand how a dog's memory works. The ability of dogs to only "live in the moment" also makes them trainable. In my 22 years of working with dogs, I have worked with thousands of them, and there have only been a few dogs that I could not help.

Scientific research on how dogs perceive time and recall events is limited. With regard to memory and time, we know dogs are different than humans. My experience tells me that dogs cannot mentally travel back in time or into the future the way we can. To be able to recall specific memories and anticipate events in the future seem like wonderful gifts, but at the same time, these human abilities come with a cost: anxiety, dread, guilt, and regret.

Many of my clients are skeptical when I tell them dogs live only in the present and that their real memory span is actually very short—about 20 seconds. After all, they argue, my dog is trained to retrieve a ball and drop it at my feet every time I throw it. They do remember what to do. But that's not what is happening in their brains.

Remember, dogs have learned how to react to commands and to please humans. So dogs can know how to respond to the command "retrieve" without having a memory of the specific event in which they learned that command. You may remember all the details of that bright spring day you taught your dog to fetch, but she doesn't. At least, not the same way you do.

A dog remembers people and places based on associations he has had with those people and places. Associative memory can work both positively and negatively. If a dog has a traumatic vet visit after a ride in the car, she may react to all car rides with fear until that memory association is replaced by associating the car ride with something positive—such as going to the dog park. The stronger the association, the harder it is to replace.

When I work with traumatized dogs, I first have to identify their negative associations. It takes time and patience to rewire these associations. I have done a lot of work with military dogs returning from war zones. Many of these dogs require extensive rewiring before they are ready for adoption into new families. Such a dog doesn't know that she is in or out of a war zone or that a war has ended. These dogs are always working and have many negative associations, usually affiliated with loud noises. The loud fireworks displays on the Fourth of July are especially difficult for these dogs.

Gavin overcame his fear of loud noises by becoming a dog again.

I worked with one special military dog named Gavin, a ten-year-old yellow Lab who was retired from the Bureau of Alcohol, Tobacco, Firearms, and Explosives (ATF).

Gavin had spent two years in Iraq, where he developed a serious noise aversion problem. When he came back to the United States, he would show fear at the sound of thunder or fireworks. The disorder progressed to include fear of high-pitched noises like smoke detectors and screams from children.

When Gavin first came to me, he didn't even know how to be with other dogs. He just froze around my pack. As part of Gavin's military training, he had become so used to a pack of people that he had forgotten how to be around dogs. It was as if he had become a robot, with all the "dog" drained out of him.

I rehabilitate these dogs by introducing an activity that is in the dogs' natural DNA but not in their daily routine. In Gavin's case, it was swimming. Labradors are natural-born swimmers, originally bred to help fishermen pull in their nets. At first, Gavin was a little hesitant, but after a few tries, he really took to the water. He regained his confidence and, in doing so, his natural dog instincts returned. Once Gavin returned to being himself, he became trainable. Rather than being fearful and distrustful of loud noises—something Gavin learned in his military life—I taught him to associate loud noise with lying down. Every time Gavin heard a loud noise, I instructed him to lie down and rest. Over time, Gavin learned to be more relaxed around noise.

Gavin was eventually adopted by his ATF agent, L. A. Bykowsky, no longer fearful of loud sounds. On days when L. A. wasn't on assignment, Gavin would come into the office to visit old friends and dogs. Sadly Gavin passed away in February 2011 after a battle with cancer, living his final years a happy, balanced dog.

▶ Stimulate the Brain, Early and Often

I am often asked if dog owners can do anything to make their dogs smarter. If you look on the supermarket shelves, you'll see numerous dog foods that claim to aid in intelligence. I don't know if diet can increase intelligence, and dogs cannot take IQ tests to prove this one way or the other. However, I do believe "stimulating" a dog during early puppyhood can result in a stronger, more balanced brain.

A puppy's brain is like a sponge—soaking up all the smells and sights and experiences in the world as fast as it can. A well-stimulated pup will grow up to have a larger brain with more cells, bigger cells, and more interconnections between them. Hearing loud noises, getting regular exercise, meeting new dogs and people, traveling to new places, and even going through agility course training for a few minutes each day make for a stronger brain. We can influence the development of a puppy's brain by providing him with the best environment possible when he is a newborn pup.

Likewise, a dog that is deprived of stimulation or that doesn't have interactions with other dogs or humans is more likely to have a smaller brain and be less balanced. I have seen many situations in which an understimulated dog is not only an unhappy dog but also a dull, almost lifeless animal.

But, conversely, too much of a good thing can be harmful. I have also seen situations in which overstimulating a dog can lead to behavior problems and aggression. Signs of overstimulation can be seen in a dog who enters a room or approaches another dog face-to-face, with his tongue hanging out, gasping for breath, and pulling on the leash or barking. A lot of dog owners misinterpret these signs as those of a "happy" dog, but in reality, such dogs are out of control. When you see these signs, your dog needs calm, deliberate handling, and it's best to move him away from whatever is overstimulating him until he has calmed down.

TECHNIQUES IN ACTION:
Challenging Your Dog's Mind

Keeping your dogs mentally challenged and constantly exposing them to new things are just as important as taking them for walks and exercising them. Bored dogs develop destructive behaviors and take their negative energy out on things like your furniture. Here are some creative ways to stimulate your dog's mind:

1. Work on a new trick. Every time you engage your dog in a training session, you are providing him with a mental challenge. Search around for new tricks to learn and practice. If you're ready to move past the basic commands of "sit," "stay," and "come" . . . try linking commands together like "retrieve and sit."

2. Play with interactive games or toys. Dog toys have evolved beyond rubber squeaky toys and cloth squirrels. I like to use canine puzzles that allow you to hide treats and objects inside the puzzle, which engage your dog in figuring out how to work them out. If you don't have a puzzle, you can hold a treat in one hand and let your dog figure out which hand is hiding the treat. Because dogs have such a powerful sense of smell, your dog will guess right 100 percent of the time.

3. Change your walk routine. Try a different street or park just to keep it interesting for your dog.

4. Give your dog a job to do. Dogs are bred to complete tasks like hunting and herding. Engage your dog in a game of

Frisbee. Get him involved in a sport like agility or flyball. Find jobs that fulfill your dog's breed.

5 Socialize your dog. Dogs are social animals, and you should nurture the need for social activity by planning playdates with other compatible dogs.

▸ Seeing Things Your Dog's Way

Most of the happiest, most well-balanced dogs that I see seem to have owners who instinctively understand them. They are able to understand the world their dog lives in and to help guide him through it. You can become that kind of Pack Leader, too. That is why it's so vital to understand how your dog's brain works, how it processes information, and how instincts can drive behavior. By having a strong grasp on all this information, you're well equipped to move on to the following chapters that build on this foundation. Being able to "see" your dog's unique point of view will help you embrace the techniques and principles to come.

CHAPTER TWO

Cesar's Natural Dog Laws

O ne of the most frequent questions that dog owners ask me is, "Just what is dog psychology?" Many
believe that dog psychology is the same as human
psychology, but it isn't. What people need to realize is that dog psychology is very different from human psychology. Rather than examining human emotions and reactions, dog
psychology tries to understand and explain dog behavior from a
canine's perspective rather than from a human one.

And to gain even more insight into a canine state of mind, you
need to understand what I call Natural Dog Laws. If you are going
to control your dogs and be their Pack Leader, you must understand who they are and what they need *as dogs* in their natural state.

So what are the Natural Dog Laws? At their core, they are the
end results of thousands of years of evolution on wild dogs. They
are fundamental truths that must be understood for dogs to live
in harmony with humans. These powerful forces still continue
to shape how modern dogs think and behave. These are the laws
that Mother Nature has placed upon the species. If you ignore
them, you will be working against Mother Nature, and she is a
powerful force to fight. The five laws are:

1. Dogs are instinctual. Humans are intellectual, emotional, and spiritual.
2. Energy is everything.
3. Dogs are first animals, then species, then breed, and then name.
4. A dog's senses form his reality.
5. Dogs are social pack animals with a leader and followers.

We will examine each of these laws and their effects on dogs' memory, behavior, and intellect. Once you understand these five laws, you can then begin to apply the Core Principles and Pack Leader Techniques discussed in Chapters 3 and 4. Put these things together, and you have the essential tools for achieving your goal—a calm, submissive dog that respects, trusts, and loves you.

In my experience, most humans focus only on the outcome: "Why won't my dog do what I say?" Some focus only on techniques—the right or wrong way to walk a dog, for instance. But without understanding the Natural Dog Laws, you will have difficulty achieving any positive outcome, no matter what technique you use. Once you've mastered the Natural Dog Laws, you'll be amazed at how simple it is to successfully apply the training techniques discussed later in the book.

FIRST NATURAL DOG LAW: Dogs Are Instinctual. Humans Are Intellectual, Emotional, and Spiritual.

One of the most frequent problems I deal with in humans is that they think their dogs are just like them. Take a look at how much people tend to humanize our dogs. We throw them birthday parties, dress them up in costumes, push them in baby carriages, and hold conversations with them as if they were our confidants.

People (at least some of them) enjoy these things. So why wouldn't their dogs? What many people don't realize is that these kinds of activities aren't fulfilling for the dog. They're fulfilling for the people. They are using the dogs for their own emotional yearnings and needs.

Another common mistake that many people make is ascribing human emotions to their dogs. How often have you heard a dog owner say, "Poor pooch, he's sad because . . ." and then he constructs an elaborate story for explaining the dog's discomfort? "He's sad because I yelled at him," or "He's sad because someone mistreated him." Typically, we use human-based emotional explanations for a dog's outward sadness or depression. Although dogs do possess emotions, the emotions are not as complex as a human's. Dogs do, however, sense the emotions coming from humans. They feel our emotions as energy, and energy to dogs is either positive or negative. Dogs read negative energy as weakness and then react accordingly.

Because we're constantly explaining dog problems in human terms, our relationships with our dogs suffer. What we fail to see time and again is that the solution we would use for a human is totally wrong for solving a dog's issues. For example, when a human sees a scared or nervous dog, he or she will first offer comfort and then try to console the frightened animal. This action can have the opposite result of reassuring the dog and making him feel more secure. The comfort and affection can actually reinforce the dog's negative behavior because it rewards it. The problem can get worse because unstable behavior has been reinforced.

Of course, this would never, ever happen in the animal world. In the animal world, an unstable pack member would be ignored by the rest of the pack. If the instability persisted or got to the point where it endangered the pack, the animal would be rejected. When a dog sees unstable energy, his instincts are almost the polar opposite of a human's first impulse.

To understand our dogs, we must always remember they are instinctual creatures. They don't think like we think, and their emotions are not like ours.

The following are some human behaviors that indicate when you are humanizing your dogs and ignoring their instincts.

CESAR'S 5 MOST COMMON WAYS PEOPLE HUMANIZE DOGS

Humanizing dogs can disrupt your dog's balance and lead to behavior issues over time. People humanize dogs in a lot of ways, but these bad habits are the most common:

1. Allowing a dog to act like a human (that is, eating at the dinner table, sleeping in a human bed)
2. Attributing human feelings and emotions to a dog's actions, body language, or facial expressions
3. Dressing dogs up in costumes that serve no protective or identification purposes

4. Expecting dogs to understand and interpret human language
5. Applying human solutions to dog problems (that is, comforting an anxious dog, or greeting an overexcited dog with enthusiasm)

SECOND NATURAL DOG LAW:
Energy Is Everything.

There has been a lot of scientific study of the effects of genetics, breeding, and evolution on dog behavior. However, there isn't enough recognition or understanding of how human energy directly affects a dog's behavior. So what exactly is energy? Energy is what I call *beingness;* it is who and what you are in every moment. Dogs use constant energy to communicate. Dogs don't recognize each other by name, but by the energy they project and the activities they share. They know humans in the same way.

As humans, we too are communicating with energy—whether or not we realize it. On the surface, our primary form of communication is language. We use our words to express ourselves. But dogs don't have words. A dog will express what's on his mind through the position of his ears and eyes and how he holds his tail or head and how he moves. These are important clues that, if not understood by humans, can lead to misunderstanding or, even worse, behavior problems. And though humans may attempt to persuade, explain, and rationalize with words all day long, we must recognize that we are projecting energy signals, the strongest messages we send to our dogs.

Many people have trouble grasping the "energy as communication" concept. I have found that this law is the hardest for humans to understand. A few years ago, I was asked to meet with a group of dog behaviorists in London to explain how energy can influence and even predict dog behavior. After an hour of conversation, I could tell there was still confusion in the room. "What do you mean by energy? How do I recognize it?"

A dog's mind works by watching our body postures and getting information about the environment through his senses—primarily smell, sight, and sound. Dogs are able to do amazing things with these "superpowers"—just think of Seeing Eye dogs and search and rescue dogs.

While I sat in this room full of learned and educated behaviorists, I asked them, "Doesn't it stand to reason that if a dog can detect bombs, drugs, or find lost humans, might this same dog be able to understand and sense our moods, emotions, and energy?"

In fact, two years prior, I had visited a cancer research center in northern California, where dogs were able to diagnose lung cancer with a 77 percent accuracy rate just by catching a whiff of a patient's breath. Surely, if a dog's sense of smell is so acute, couldn't she also potentially sense our states of mind? I believe that most dogs can.

When I think about these questions of energy, it brings to mind one of the most important experiences in my life, when I relied on my dog Daddy's instincts and energy to make an important decision for our pack.

When Daddy, my first right-hand dog, was nearing the end of his life, I began looking for a new pack member that Daddy would be able to teach and integrate into my pack. Daddy had shared my life and work since he was four months old. Working with me, Daddy became used to being around dogs of all sizes. This exposure and his natural balanced energy made him a perfect candidate for rehabilitating other dogs, particularly those with dog aggression issues. Daddy's calm, submissive energy was contagious. I trusted him implicitly. And it was vital to me that I seek out another dog to carry on his legacy.

My friend had a pit bull who had just had a litter of puppies, and Daddy and I went to meet them. I watched carefully how the puppies interacted with their mother and with each other.

One puppy in particular caught my eye. It was obvious he was the pick of the litter—strong, handsome, and with beautiful markings. I brought my pick over to Daddy and, to my surprise, Daddy growled at him. I then selected another puppy that I liked. He was all white and had a wide head, but Daddy totally ignored him.

Then I saw another puppy. He was the closest to his mother and had a gorgeous, solid blue coat. I picked him up and set him down near Daddy. Daddy approached the pup, and the two dogs went nose to nose. Then Daddy wagged his tail, turned around, and—to my utter surprise—the puppy followed Daddy to the car and never looked back at his mother. That was the pup who became Junior. Daddy and Junior knew they were right for each other. It was pure instincts and energy.

In the months and years to follow, Daddy trained Junior. (The only thing I did was potty-train Junior, a chore Daddy chose not to participate in.)

As it turned out, Daddy knew what was best for me. Junior has the perfect energy for the pack, and he was ideally suited for his mission of helping me rehabilitate dogs. I trusted Daddy and I relied on his instincts to pick his successor. If you want to

Daddy showed Junior the importance of a good nap.

relate to dogs, you must live in their world. It's an instinctual world—not an intellectual or spiritual world. You enter this world by trusting your instincts.

The scientific community is just now starting to examine the effects of energy on behavior. Of course, most of what I know about dogs is based on a lifetime of working with them. So, it's always rewarding for me when academics publish a new scientific study on dog behavior in which the studies confirm, or at least support, the beliefs and observations I've developed over a lifetime.

In February 2012, *Current Biology* published results from a research study conducted at the Cognitive Development Center of the Central European University in Budapest, Hungary, which indicates that dogs can respond to eye contact and nonverbal cues from humans in a similar manner as two-year-old human children.

In the study, dogs were able to read nonverbal cues, especially when the humans used eye contact. Nicholas Dodman, the director of the Animal Behavior Clinic at Tufts University's Cummings School of Veterinary Medicine in North Grafton, Massachusetts, summarized some of the research by saying, "Dogs are looking for an expression of what the person is thinking."

This study confirms what I have always believed, that dogs are more attuned to our energy and nonverbal behaviors than we might think. Dogs can read energy better than they can understand the tone and inflection in our voice. They understand our body language more than our human language.

THIRD NATURAL DOG LAW:
Dogs Are First Animal, Then Species, Then Breed, and Then Name.

Now that we have an understanding of energy, we can begin to put all the pieces together for a complete picture of the dog. But not all pieces are equal—we must put them in their proper order.

Dogs are first **animal,** then **species,** then **breed,** and finally they have a **name.** Humans often make the mistake of thinking of this backward, starting with their dog's name and failing to identify them, at their core, as an animal.

HOW BEHAVIOR IS UNDERSTOOD AND EXPLAINED

HUMAN PSYCHOLOGY	Name → Breed → Species → Animal
DOG PSYCHOLOGY	Animal → Species → Breed → Name

In dog psychology, a dog is an animal first and foremost. It is not a human. When we relate to our dogs, especially when trying to correct an unwanted behavior, it's important to think of them first as an animal (mammal), then as a species (dog, or *Canis lupus familiaris*), then as a unique breed (German shepherd, husky, and so on) with certain characteristics or skills, and last and least important, as their name (personality). To have a happy, balanced dog is to respect these qualities about them—in this order.

Let's take each of these words and examine why they work in the order I've placed them.

When I think of **animal,** I think nature, the wilderness, and freedom. Animals live in the present, and life is simple. They live purely in the moment and know only their immediate needs. Animals are instinctual. They are not intellectual or spiritual. Their basic needs are shelter, food, water, and mating. So, in thinking about your dog, think about her the way a dog does. First, basic needs are foremost. Satisfying these needs is the strongest motivational factor in a dog's life.

Next is **species.** Dogs were descended from wolves. This species is concerned with pack orientation, communicating and experiencing the world through senses, and understanding pack positioning and leadership. All dogs need to play a role in a pack. They need a job. They can be protectors, hunters, or searchers. Once you understand their instinctual needs as a species, you might begin to understand dogs' frustration when they only get to walk a couple of blocks around their neighborhood a couple of times a week. Their frustration is innate, and they develop behavioral issues to compensate.

Third is **breed.** After humans domesticated dogs, they began to breed them to favor specific genetic traits and abilities. Breeds are mostly a human creation. In my formula, breed represents the characteristics that we have genetically altered or enhanced so that certain dogs perform certain tasks better than others. For instance, bloodhounds are incredible scent trackers; greyhounds are amazing sprinters; border collies are very intelligent; and German shepherds are good at guarding.

Today, these are almost all human-desired tasks, like herding, searching, and stalking. These different traits can affect a dog's psychology and energy. Within breeds, there are different levels of energy—high-, medium-, and low-energy dogs that take to their breed-specific tasks with different levels of intensity.

There are definite differences in the intelligence and traits of various breeds, and there is also a lot of individual variation among dogs of the same breed. Although we are often quick to generalize among breeds, we must remember that breed alone doesn't do a good job of explaining how dogs behave or how "trainable" they are, which is why it appears third on this list.

Finally, your dog has a **name**. Your dog does not know or need to know the difference of whether you call him or her Sam, Fiona, or Fido. A name is a human creation that we condition our dog to learn. We use names to project personality on the dogs, but what "personality" is to a human doesn't exist in dog psychology. It doesn't exist in either the animal, species, or breed categories. Naming your Doberman pinscher "Rambo" will not make him aggressive, just as calling a Yorkshire terrier "Baby" won't mean that she will be docile and happy to lie down all day like an infant.

Recognizing these four categories—in this order—and understanding their influences on behavior are a central part of having a happy, balanced dog.

FOURTH NATURAL DOG LAW:
A Dog's Senses Form His Reality.

In Chapter 1, we covered the fundamentals of how a dog's brain and his inborn instincts shape his unique view of the world. We learned that a dog senses the world very differently than a human does, so the world a dog experiences is much different than what we experience. To understand a dog's mind, we have to enter a different instinctual world, as it is formed by his senses.

Humans experience the world primarily through sight; they see a colorful, vibrant world. But dogs sense the world primarily through smell, followed by sight in shades of gray—like watching black-and-white TV. Because the sensory experiences of humans and canines are so distinct from each other, how could a dog and human ever experience the same world? What we *see*, we experience. What a dog *smells*, he experiences. Humans see each other first and begin to form opinions and likes based on what they see. Dogs smell a human, usually from distances greater than 50 yards away, and begin to develop an understanding of who that person is based on smell.

HIERARCHY OF SENSORY INPUTS TO THE BRAIN

HUMAN HIERARCHY	CANINE HIERARCHY
1. Sight	1. Smell
2. Touch	2. Sight
3. Sound	3. Sound
4. Smell	4. Touch

These fundamental differences between the senses of a dog and a human help to explain one of the most irrational behaviors I've seen humans do when they see a dog for the first time. They immediately run up to a new dog and lean down to try to pet her. Humans do this because touch is their second strongest sense. But I guarantee you, if dogs could talk, they would be saying, "Human, get out of my face, I don't know you yet."

I was once asked to comment on a story about a Denver news anchor named Kyle Dyer that aired on the *Today* show. Kyle, a dog lover, was covering a story about a dramatic rescue by firemen of an Argentine mastiff who had fallen into an icy lake. During the news segment, Kyle had been petting and stroking the dog. As the interview ended, she leaned in close to the dog's face to say goodbye. Unfortunately, the dog bit her while she was still on the air. After several surgeries to repair the damage to her lip and nose, Kyle returned to her job with a different sense of how to interact with an unfamiliar dog. She admitted on the *Today* show that it was likely she made a mistake: "Maybe I was too close; maybe he was unsettled."

This mistake is repeated thousands of times a day because humans love to touch, but I have a simple, more respectful technique for meeting a dog for the first time. The "No Touch, No Talk, No Eye Contact" approach gives dogs a chance to smell you and get to know you first before they allow you to enter their personal space.

When using the "No Touch, No Talk, No Eye Contact" approach, first remember to keep your energy calm and assertive. Focus on the people around you and ignore the dog as she sniffs at your feet and legs. Keep your hands to yourself, and ignore the dog. Don't look at the dog and don't talk to her. Let her get to know you first. When she has the information she's looking for, she will either walk away from you or enter into a calm, submissive state and move around to face you.

Before you turn your attention to the dog, be sure to ask the dog's owner for permission to engage with the dog. At this point, look at the dog and speak to her. If she approaches, offer your closed fist, fingers up, for a sniff. If she is showing no signs of anxiety or aggression, then you can pet her, although it's always a good idea to first touch a strange dog by scratching its chest or the side of its shoulder. Some dogs can perceive a touch from above on the head or neck as aggression. As you are getting to know each other, the safest touch is the smartest.

"No Touch, No Talk, No Eye Contact" can be used in a lot of situations. For instance, it's effective for dealing with your own dogs when they are overexcited or anxious. If your dog starts to jump or spin excitedly when you return home, then "No Touch, No Talk, No Eye Contact" will teach him that you will not reward such excited behavior with your attention. If you are consistent and do not acknowledge your dog until he has reached a calm, submissive state, then you can minimize or eliminate the hyperactive greeting upon your return.

It is also important to teach visitors to your home to follow the "No Touch, No Talk, No Eye Contact" approach. It's very common for people to say that they don't mind when their friends' dogs jump up on them, but in your house, you must be consistent with the rules. Your dog should not be allowed to jump up on you or your family members, so he must not be allowed to jump up on other humans. It can also give you peace of mind by avoiding situations that might escalate because someone does not know how to approach a dog properly.

FIFTH NATURAL DOG LAW:
Dogs Are Social Pack Animals With a Leader and Followers.

Understanding how dogs have evolved over thousands of years to become our lifelong companions is a big part of understanding how dogs behave. Mother Nature selected the dog to be the one species that would be culled from the wild and chosen to become man's best friend. Dogs did this by figuring out ways to help humans. From helping us to hunt, herd, and protect to becoming symbols of wealth, status, and nobility, dogs became— and remained— humans' favorite animal.

Evidence of fossil remains and genetic study support the belief that modern dogs are descended from a small subspecies of wolves that lived in the Near East approximately 20,000 years ago. The domestic dog has 78 chromosomes, the same number as the wolf. Dogs were probably first domesticated from several different breeds of wolf. Over the ages, these animals were bred with different types of wild wolves and wild dog hybrids, which changed their gene pool and led to the great genetic variations of today's dogs.

The modern-day dog doesn't look the least bit like his ancestral wolf. Human breeding has meant that, through evolution, dogs have smaller teeth and shorter jaws than wolves, resulting in a decreased ability to catch and kill prey. But dogs did inherit the social organization evident in wolf packs.

Wolf packs work as a group, with all individuals in the pack working toward the same goal. For the group to function at its best, pack society has always allowed different personalities to develop. Everyone has a part to play: One wolf might be the best

Two distant cousins: A gray wolf and a Maltese pose for a "family" portrait.

hunter, while another might be the most strategic or best defender.

This "pack" mentality is evident not just in wolves and dogs. Humans also have some of the same social structures evidenced in packs, including role definition for various "pack" members and cooperative problem solving. It's important that you play the role of Pack Leader in your home and project calm, assertive energy. If the Pack Leader role is absent, it will only be a matter of time before your dog or something else assumes that role.

One afternoon, I was teaching a class in pack leadership to a group of 40 students at the DPC when one woman with a Jack Russell terrier caught my attention. Her dog was out of control and wanted to chase everything that moved in the classroom. The poor woman was so focused on maintaining control of her dog that she was missing the class instruction. I called her and her dog up to the front of the room. I then used a turtle we had at the center to illustrate my lesson in pack behavior. The dog tried to attack the turtle. The Jack Russell would not relent; time and again, he lunged after the poor slow-moving turtle who just wanted to get as far away as possible from this high-strung, aggressive dog. I then tied the dog's leash around the turtle, and the turtle began to pull the dog forward. An amazing thing began to happen. The dog started to follow the turtle, and the turtle's slow, deliberate energy seemed to transfer over to the dog, who seemed calmer and less agitated. The lesson for the class was that, in the absence of a strong Pack Leader, dogs will either become the pack leader themselves or allow other animals or people to become their leader for them.

Packs have roles, and they have an order. One of the most common causes of canine instability occurs when a human inadvertently changes the natural order of the pack. A person may take a low-energy, happy-go-lucky dog that is content being in the back of the pack and try to make him a pack leader or a guard dog, or give him some other role for which the dog is unsuited. How often have you heard the complaint that "A stranger could walk over my dog before he took notice or barked"? What these people fail to recognize is that their dog's role is not to be the protector, and thus they unfairly push against instinct and natural order. The important takeaway is to know your dog and know his position in the pack.

All of these Natural Dog Laws form the very foundation of your life with a happy dog. Be mindful of instincts and energy. Understand your dog's unique place in the world. Honor his senses. And respect your dog's need for a pack. By recognizing and embracing these five simple laws, you will put yourself in the right frame of mind to see your dog for the amazing creature that he is. Now that you can recognize that, it's time to find balance.

CHAPTER THREE

Nine Simple Principles for a Balanced Dog

A happier life with your dog becomes easy to achieve once you see your dog as a dog and honor his unique canine perspective. Now you're truly able to appreciate the differences in the way humans and dogs perceive and interact with the world. And armed with the knowledge, you can move into the proper position as Pack Leader.

When I combined my understanding of a dog's brain with acceptance of the Natural Dog Laws, a powerful set of Core Principles emerged. These key lessons are my secret weapon in creating balance for any Pack Leader—from those who've had dogs for years to those who are just starting out. Regardless of their experience, humans must see that a balanced dog lives as she would in nature—knowing her place within the pack, knowing what is expected of her, and exhibiting calm, submissive energy. She follows her Pack Leader and doesn't misbehave. To get there, humans must observe and practice these nine Core Principles. These instinctual tools lie at the center of creating a balanced life for you, your family, and your dog.

When you achieve the goal of bringing your dog into balance, you will experience an entirely different relationship. You will be able to communicate instinctually and understand each other's needs. You and your dog will be in tune with each other in a much deeper, more rewarding way, and you will learn the benefits of bringing calm, assertive energy into all aspects of your life.

CORE PRINCIPLE #1:
Be Aware of Your Energy.

In Chapter 2, we learned that energy is everything. It's the way in which humans and animals present themselves to the world, and it is exhibited through body language, facial expression, and eye contact (or lack thereof). In humans, it is a secondary form of communication, after language, but in dogs, it is the primary form of communication. One dog can assert dominance over another by simply moving in with calm, assertive energy and claiming the space. Dogs do not say "excuse me," "please," or "thank you" in words. If they maintain calm, assertive energy, they do not need to.

Humans do have words, though, and we rely on them, whether we are communicating in conversation or in writing. Because of our intellectual capacity for speech, it is very easy for us to lose touch with our own energy, and to have no idea what we are projecting to the world. However, despite our dependence on language, we do pick up on each other's energy, whether or not we know it, and this does affect our message. Have you ever heard someone give a speech in a flat, unenthusiastic monotone? No matter how stirring and well written the words, such a speaker would quickly bore his audience to death. Conversely, someone who presents a confident, enthusiastic energy can easily persuade a group of people to go along with the stupidest idea ever conceived. Why? Because, again, their energy exerts an influence on the listeners, whether or not they are aware of it.

Quite often, when I'm working with clients, they have no idea that they're projecting nervous or weak energy until I point it out to them. They are not in tune with their own energy at all, and so have no idea why their dog is reacting to them in the way he does. But, because dogs communicate primarily with energy, they can read a human in a second. I'm sure you've noticed that some people naturally draw dogs to themselves, and others cause dogs to flee on sight. Dogs will always be attracted to calm, assertive energy. Likewise, they will always try to avoid weak, nervous, or unbalanced energy.

To be successful as the Pack Leader—and as a person in general—you need to be mindful of your energy and learn to adjust it when you are not in a calm, assertive mode. Take a moment right now and pay attention to how you're feeling emotionally, then notice how you're holding your body. Usually, your body language will reflect your emotional state whether or not you're aware of it. If you're feeling nervous or upset at this moment, then your body is probably tense. If you're feeling insecure, then you are probably hunched over or slouching.

Body language can influence your emotional state, and you can go a long way toward developing calm, assertive energy by being aware of your posture. Stand straight, with your head up, shoulders back, and chest out. Keep both feet flat on the ground. Try to avoid crossing your arms or shoving your hands in your pockets. Breathe deeply and exhale slowly. Stand like this for a few minutes, focusing on your breathing while trying to clear your mind of random thoughts. If it is safe to do so, close your eyes and concentrate on what you can smell and hear. You should find yourself calming down naturally. Remember the feeling and the body language, and then practice being able to move into this mode of being upon demand.

In nature, when a dog in a pack shows excited or unbalanced energy, the entire pack takes it as a warning of impending danger. It is remarkable how quickly a sleeping pack of dogs will fire up and go on high alert when one dog barks, and just as remarkable how quickly they settle down when the Pack Leader determines that there is no threat and goes back into a calm, assertive state. When dealing with your dog, you can see the importance, then, of not going into an unstable energy state. To do so is to send the message that something is wrong. You may not even be aware of the messages you are sending to your dog. This is why it is so important to become aware of your own energy and then take control of it. Until you can control yourself, you cannot control your dog.

CORE PRINCIPLE #2:
Live in the Moment.

Humans are probably unique among animals in their ability to daydream and fantasize, and we do it constantly. While reading this book, you may have remembered what you had for breakfast, or reminded yourself to buy lightbulbs next time you're out. If you haven't recently, then you probably just did, or you are right now—and if you're not careful, you're going to have to reread the rest of this paragraph because you became lost in your own thoughts. I'll wait for you to go back and catch up.

I'm not sure whether there is any evolutionary advantage to the human tendency to live in the past, present, and future simultaneously, but I'm pretty sure we do it because of our highly developed language skills. We may relive our best moments, or dream about an ideal vacation, or rehearse the speech we're going to give to our boss in hopes of a raise.

This is not to suggest that animals do not have a connection to the past or future. A dog that once ate onions and became very sick may forever after flee at the mere smell of an onion. A squirrel hoarding nuts in its nest is aware that they are to be eaten at a later time, but he is not consciously thinking, "This will be dinner next Tuesday evening."

In both cases, past and future are minor influences on what's happening right now. After the bad experience of an onion, the dog does not go through the mental steps of "I smell onion. Oh, I remember the time I ate that onion and felt really bad. I better run away now." The thought process is instinctual and instant. The experience of the onion left enough of an impression that the stimulus induces flight with no logical process behind it. Similarly, the dog does not spend her time thinking, "I really hope I don't come across any onions today." The dog doesn't have any thoughts of an onion until it again becomes a present reality in the here and now.

As humans, we forget that dogs live in the moment, and this can be an impediment to rehabilitation and training. Dogs that have lost a limb, hearing, or sight do not lament the abilities that are gone. They deal with the abilities they still have, and they don't waste time feeling sorry for themselves. With our human obsession with the past, we are the ones who relive a dog's former traumas and then overload them with sympathy and affection that, in the dog's mind, is unearned.

Dogs do not hold grudges or brood about the past. Even in the case of two dogs that do not get along and fight when in sight of each other, some remembered incident of the past does not set off another fight. Rather, the sight of the other dog triggers the instinctual recall, but even then, the dogs may not fight until one of them interprets the other as doing something that is aggressive. Once a fight is over, they have no hard feelings, and neither plans how to kill the other in his sleep. Contrast that to human grudges, where an insult (real or imagined) can lead to years of enmity and bad feelings.

This natural living in the moment is what makes it possible to rehabilitate dogs. Because they do not cling to the past or worry about the future, they are open-minded and constantly learning in the present. They do not resent being corrected or disciplined because, once it's over, it's over. They associate it with the moment it happened, and then they let go.

This is one of the most powerful lessons we can learn from dogs. Being obsessed with the past or future can lead to many negative emotions: resentment, regret, anxiety, fear, or envy. Letting go of what is over and done, and of what we cannot control, is the path to our own fulfillment in the here and now. It is also one more way of being that will help you to have a balanced relationship with your dog.

CORE PRINCIPLE #3:
Dogs Don't Lie.

During the filming of the *Dog Whisperer,* I worked with so many families on rehabilitating more than 400 of their dogs. Before I met any of these people, I asked my production crew not to tell me what the problem or situation was. Having a clean slate when I first encountered the dog and talked with the family was essential for figuring out the root of the problem in the household. In almost every instance, the people typically told me the "story" about what was going on, but the dogs told me the "truth." A dog's energy is nothing but honest. By just observing the dog, I can get a good sense of what the situation really is.

We humans have a great ability to tell stories, and so we tell them to ourselves. Please don't misunderstand me. I don't think any of these people were being willfully dishonest about their feelings or emotions, or what they perceived the problem to be. They weren't doing it to be malicious, but rather to protect themselves. When humans don't accept the truth about what's going on inside them, it becomes more difficult to help their dogs. The most difficult cases I encounter are the ones where the human is in denial and attributing a complex explanation to his dog's misbehavior. The only cases I was not able to solve were those in which the humans never overcame their denial.

I was explaining the difference between "truth" and "story" to a group of students who were attending the Training Cesar's Way class in fundamentals at the Dog Psychology Center. To illustrate my point, I decided to use a real-life situation. There was a woman in the class we'll call "Ann." She has a therapy dog named "Monarch," one of the most gentle and sensitive dogs you'll ever meet. These are the very qualities that make him perfect for the job.

Ann said, "Monarch and I have a communication problem. He doesn't always do what I tell him to do, and he is very timid when I give him direction." This was Ann's human story about what was happening. But her body language and her energy told a different one.

It was obvious to the other students that Ann was overly concerned about how Monarch was reacting to her. Her eyes darted down at Monarch to see his every reaction. She didn't move deliberately and with confidence. She held on to the leash with very little slack so Monarch had to stay close by her side. She was overcompensating for Monarch's perceived indifference to her commands.

The truth behind the situation was that Ann didn't trust Monarch, and Monarch knew it. Now, think for a moment, would you follow a person or leader you knew didn't trust you? Ann was too timid, too fearful, and she was projecting that energy to her dog. Because Monarch is a trained therapy dog, he is extra sensitive to humans, and especially sensitive to Ann's behavior.

When I took Monarch's leash, I held it very lightly with two fingers. Confidently and calmly, I walked Monarch through non-verbal commands that I gave with body movements. He followed without hesitation. Then I took off the leash entirely, and Monarch suddenly came to life. What was once a timid and tentative therapy dog was now a happy but calm, submissive creature. He performed every command with pleasure. The class applauded, and Monarch sat on his hind legs and then rolled over on his back—the ultimate sign of submission and confidence. Ann needed to get beyond her story and work with the truth—only then was she really able to help her dog.

You can practice dissecting the difference between story and truth with a friend or spouse. Write down what you think is the cause of a situation or upset within your household. Next, engage in an honest discussion about the causes of the upset. Write them down for everyone to see and examine. Peel away the causes like an onion until you get to the cold, hard truth about what's really going on and what's really causing the upset. Although this exercise can be intimidating, the end result will be freedom and release. In many of the *Dog Whisperer* cases in which people did overcome their denial, their stories usually ended with human tears, sighs of relief, and a rehabilitated dog.

✓ CORE PRINCIPLE #4:
Work With Mother Nature, Not Against Her.

I discussed this earlier in Chapter 2, but it's always worth repeating. We need to consider a dog in this order: animal, species, breed, and then name. The first two are a part of what a dog is naturally, while humans created the last two. Animals live in and deal with nature every day. To be successful and survive, all animals—from rats to eagles—need to follow the laws of nature. We humans have forgotten nature's laws because we have protected ourselves from the consequences of breaking them, but that doesn't mean we are exempt.

If you live in a modern, First or Second World country, it can be very easy to lose touch with nature. Your home protects you from the elements. You probably travel from home to your job in a car or on some form of public transportation. Your next meal is as close as the refrigerator, the grocery store, or the restaurant down the street. The only times you probably really notice nature are when the weather is unpleasant, or when you're picking up after your dog on the walk.

None of this is natural for a dog, and yet we have transplanted these wild pack animals into our homes. In nature, a dog's life is very simple. Because dogs' realities are formed primarily by the senses, they live moment by moment, and everything is focused on what they need to survive—shelter, food, water, and, in season, mating. They roam their territory with their pack in search of fulfilling those needs. Dogs do not worry about the future or dwell on the past. They exist in the moment, which can be something very difficult for humans to understand, especially with the stresses of modern life. Remember, we form our reality through beliefs, knowledge, and memory.

If you really want to learn what it's like to live in the moment, try being homeless for a few months. I was when I first came to the United States, and it's interesting how quickly you stop living in the past or dreaming of the future when your biggest concerns are where your next meal will come from and where you will sleep that night. When I describe it that way, it sounds like every dog would appreciate living in a home with a constant supply of food, but dogs cannot rationalize their instincts like humans can. You can take a dog out of nature, but you cannot take nature out of a dog.

As a species, dogs are a specific kind of animal that deals with nature in particular ways, having inherited their pack nature from wolves. On the species level, dogs are different than deer, tigers, llamas—and humans. Their needs revolve around the pack's needs, and the pack will follow only a calm, balanced leader. Any members of the pack that become unstable are quickly dealt with, corrected if possible, and killed or banished if not.

This is why stable leadership is so important to a dog, in addition to physical needs being met. The need for leadership is programmed in a dog's genes, and exists at a primal, instinctual level. When species or animals are cut off from nature by being domesticated, it is especially important that their needs, physical and psychological, are being fulfilled. If you don't feed a dog, it will starve to death. If you don't fulfill a dog's need for leadership and direction, it will experience the canine equivalent of human neurosis, and possibly even insanity.

Dogs need to maintain their connection with nature, and we can help them do that by remaining aware of the Natural Dog Laws from Chapter 2. The wonderful part of this, though, is that we can also connect, through our dogs, to the instinctual part of ourselves with which we have lost touch. Find some place away from the modern world, even if it's just a large city park, and then go for a walk with your pack and experience the world as your dog does, forming his reality through his senses. Reconnecting with Mother Nature will bring balance to your pack, as you and your dog learn from each other.

CORE PRINCIPLE #5:
Honor Your Dog's Instincts.

I've written about dogs as animal and dogs as species, the two natural aspects of their being. But breed, one of the two human-created aspects, has a powerful part to play in shaping your dog's instincts. Breeds came about through selective mating, and the diversity of dog breeds is astounding, ranging from tiny toy dogs like Yorkies and Chihuahuas on one end all the way up to giant breeds like Great Danes and Saint Bernards. It's sometimes hard to believe that such diverse animals are even from the same species. Breeds were created for different reasons—some dogs were bred as companions, some as herders, and some as protectors. But each was bred to draw out and focus on desired instincts to create dogs that excelled at particular tasks.

Now, although the animal and species aspects of dogs are common to all of them, breed can sometimes affect behavior, and it is also sometimes necessary to consider breed when working with a dog, whether just for training, by giving them an appropriate job, or in rehabilitation. However, keep in mind that the breed is "only the suit." The more purebred a dog is, the stronger the dog will show breed characteristics and instincts. But by fulfilling her animal and species needs through the walk and using my fulfillment formula, you will minimize breed-related misbehaviors.

This doesn't mean you need to ignore breed entirely. In fact, it can be a nice experience for dogs and humans to engage in breed-appropriate activities. In cases of misbehavior caused by breed-related instincts, it is essential.

Seven basic groups of dogs—sporting, hound, working, herding, terrier, toy, and nonsporting—have been bred over the centuries for various functions. You can fulfill each of their specific needs in slightly different ways.

Dogs in the sporting group were bred to assist with hunting, by either pointing at or flushing out prey, or retrieving kills, particularly waterfowl. Good activities for this group include games that simulate finding or retrieving prey. For pointers, you

Games that involve pointing will appeal to this dog's natural sporting instincts.

can introduce them to an object with a familiar scent, and then hide it. Reward them when they "point," although don't let them actually retrieve the object, because this can stimulate their prey drive. For spaniels, let them locate the object. For retrievers, allow them to bring it to you.

Dogs in the hound group were also bred for hunting, except that unlike those in the sporting group, hounds actually do the hunting and pursuing, and their prey are usually mammals rather than birds. Hounds are divided into two groups: scent hounds and sight hounds. You can fulfill the needs of the former with the "runaway" game. This involves presenting your dog with items of clothing with familiar scents from the human pack on them, and then hiding them along a regular route of your walk. Reward your dog for every item she finds.

Sight hounds, which are accustomed to hunting from a farther distance, are natural runners, so they are ideal candidates for towing you on in-line skates or running with you on your bike. Keep in mind, though, that sight hounds are sprinters, not long-distance runners, so get used to a short, fast dash followed by a more regular-paced walk.

Dogs in the working group were bred when humans moved from a hunting-and-gathering lifestyle into villages, and their name is a pretty good description of their purpose. These dogs were used for their size and strength—for guarding, pulling, and rescuing. Naturally, these dogs excel at pulling, and letting them tow a cart on the walk is an ideal use of this instinct. Remember, working dogs do not look at pulling as a chore. It is a physical and psychological challenge that makes them feel useful and valued.

The herding group, with its instinct to control the movements of other animals, is naturally excellent at herding. However, if you don't have a herd of sheep or cattle handy, don't worry. These breeds are also excellent at agility training and, oddly enough, are world-champion flying disc (or Frisbee) dogs.

Dogs in the terrier group were bred to chase down small prey, frequently following rodents into their burrows to kill them. Although smaller, they were bred down from working and herding dogs, so many of the same activities that fulfill those breeds will work for terriers, particularly those with high energy.

The toy group dogs may have originally been bred to hunt very small animals, but evidence indicates that they quickly became just companion animals; the image of a rich woman with a teacup terrier in her purse is nothing new, and this group stemmed from the human tendency to fall in love with animals that are cute and that resemble juvenile forms. With their tiny faces and large eyes, toy dogs fit this description perfectly. Although members of the toy group have been bred from various other groups, they were not bred for any specific tasks. That is why it is even more important with toy dogs that you treat them as animals and dogs first. This group, more than any other, contains the dogs that should be allowed to be dogs. You're not doing your toy dog any favors by carrying her everywhere or letting her go off leash. Let your dog out of the bag and put a leash on her, so she can be a dog and walk around on her own feet.

Finally, the nonsporting group is somewhat of a catchall description that could have also been called "none of the above." This group includes the poodle, bulldog, Boston terrier, bichon frise, French bulldog, Lhasa apso, shar-pei, chow chow, Shiba Inu, and Dalmatian. Depending on the specific breed, you can find an appropriate activity among the preceding groups.

Although dog breeds are diverse and were created to carry out various tasks, remember that all dogs require some form of exercise, preferably via the walk. The suggestions here are designed for further bonding opportunities with your dog, as well as suggested routes for rehabilitation if you are still having issues, particularly those influenced by your dog's natural instincts.

CORE PRINCIPLE #6:
"Nose, Eyes, Ears" — in That Order.

As we have learned, dogs are instinctual, and their reality is formed by their senses; a dog's strongest sense is her sense of smell, followed by sight, then hearing, and this follows the order in which these senses develop in a puppy. Dogs learn the most about the world through their nose. We have also learned that humans approach the world through sight first and smell last, which makes it very easy for us to forget this principle. However, this is one of the most important things to remember in all of your dealings with any dogs, whether or not they are in your own pack.

Humans and dogs have shared space for so long—10,000 or possibly 20,000 years—that it is almost second nature for humans to greet new dogs the same way they do other people. I'm sure most of you have done it. You visit a friend's house and meet his new dog for the first time, and you greet the dog with a big hello and a pat on the head the second you're in the door. Maybe you even lean over to let her lick your face. After all, it would be rude to just ignore the dog, wouldn't it?

Actually, no. If you ignore a new dog at first, you're not being rude. Instead, you're being considerate of her needs. After all, you're a new person, and that can be intimidating to a dog. When you first enter her territory, she doesn't know whether you're a friend or an enemy. A well-balanced dog will look to her Pack Leader for clues and act accordingly. At the same time, she will try to figure you out through her senses—through Nose, Eyes, Ears, in that order.

The first thing she is likely to do is sniff the feet of a new human she encounters. By doing this, the dog is learning your scent and sensing your energy. While the dog is checking you out, practic-ing "No Touch, No Talk, No Eye Contact" will make sure the meeting goes smoothly. This practice respects the way the dog perceives the world, as well as respects her space, and it gives her time to explore you first (see Chapter 2, page 45).

It is very important to remember and use this Core Principle, as it affects almost every interaction you will have with your dog—from the first time you meet to your daily comings and goings at home. But take a moment to observe your dog on the walk—see what she responds to. How does an interesting smell affect her body and energy? What kinds of sights and sounds engage her? You will learn so much about your dog just through this careful observation—and the more you know about your dog and how she sees the world, the better Pack Leader you can be for her.

Core Principle #7:
Accept Your Dog's Natural Pack Position.

In nature, there are three positions in the dog pack—in the front, in the middle, and in the back—and each dog will gravitate to its natural position. The weaker dogs will wind up at the rear, and the more dominant dogs in the middle. The pack leaders are always in front.

Each position has its own function within the pack. Dogs in the three positions work together to find food and water, and ensure the pack's survival by defending the pack against danger. The dogs in front (including the leader) provide direction and protection to the pack. They determine where the entire pack will go, and they fend off any dangers from the front. The dogs in the rear are primarily concerned with alerting to danger approaching from behind, and their function is to warn the rest of the pack. The dogs in the middle are mediators, communicating between the rear and the front.

Every function is important. Without the dogs in the front, the dogs at the rear don't know where they're going. Without the dogs

The Pack Leader should be in front, with the dogs alongside or behind.

in the back, the dogs up front are not aware of any problems coming up from behind. And without the dogs in the middle to relay messages, the front and back of the pack are isolated from each other.

The canine pack leader may be able to smell that fresh water and available prey are on the other side of a dark and scary forest, and move onward toward it. Meanwhile, the dogs at the rear know only that they are all entering a dark and scary forest. Their normal reaction would be to alert to danger and start barking. The dogs in the middle sense the calm energy from the front of the pack, and they in turn calm the frightened dogs at the rear through their own calm energy. However, if the pack is being stalked from the rear by a large threat, the dogs in the rear will remain agitated and continue to alert to danger. The dogs in the middle, in turn, will pick up on this energy and communicate it to the front. The pack leader will turn the pack around to provide protection against this new threat.

By communicating through energy and having an established hierarchy, the entire pack functions as one unit. Each dog knows his place within that hierarchy, and there is no jumping around. A dog that naturally gravitates to the rear of the pack will not try to move to the middle or front, and a dog in front will not give up her position without being forced to by another dog; this generally will not happen unless that lead dog becomes unstable.

As responsible dog lovers, it is up to us to learn where our dog would normally position herself in the pack. By observing her energy and body language, you can see where your dog might most likely fit in. It is also up to us to respect our dog's own position in the pack and not try to change it—because we can't. It would violate the Natural Dog Law: Dogs are social, pack animals with a leader and followers. If you try to put a dog from the rear or middle in a leadership position (or force him to lead because no one else is doing it), the dog will become unbalanced.

The vast majority of dogs are not born to be a pack leader, and these dogs, if raised properly by humans, will never try to assume that leadership position. When you do not understand and respect your dog's position in the pack—either by trying to change it actively, or forcing the dog to change by not providing leadership—then you are not working with Mother Nature, and the outcome will not be pleasant for you or your dog.

Core Principle #8: You Create the Calm, Submissive State.

The point of the previous seven rules is to bring your dog to a place of calm, submissive energy. I'll show you how to do that in more depth in the next chapter. Everything begins with you, though, and if there is one thing that is most important in this process, it is your energy, your state of mind, and your approach. You are the source of your dog's calm, submissive state, and your dog is looking to you for guidance. If your energy is anxious, nervous, overexcited, angry, frustrated, or some other negative, then your dog will reflect back that energy. If you are inconsistent in applying your rules, then your dog will begin to test you to see what she can get away with. But if you are calm and assertive in your energy and consistent in teaching and enforcing your rules, you will earn your dog's trust, and she will follow you and look to you for guidance.

If you are having trouble mastering calm, assertive energy yourself, you may find it helpful to create an intention in your head, and then imagine it happening. For example, if your dog pulls on the walk, see yourself walking with your dog next to or just behind you and imagine what that feels like. What is your state of mind without having to constantly pull your dog back? How much more enjoyable for both of you is the walk this way?

You can also connect with your dog and help you both achieve a calm state by meditating together. To do so, sit or lie down with your dog, then place one hand on her chest and the other on her back, near her hindquarters. Pay attention to your dog's breathing, and then begin to mimic it. Breathe together for as long as you're comfortable. After a few days, your dog should start mimicking your breathing and the two of you should find a connection in those moments. Meditation in general is also calming for both of you.

Most of all, don't be intimidated. This may seem like a lot of information to take in, but start simply, and build on each successful moment. The more often you succeed, the more confident you will be in continued success and the less discouraged you will be by

Embrace being a Pack Leader, and your dog will follow.

a setback. Remember, though: You are not the only one who wants to succeed at reaching a calm, assertive state and achieving balance with your dog. Your dog wants you to succeed, too.

CORE PRINCIPLE #9:
You Need to Be the Pack Leader.

Everything comes back to these four words: "Be the Pack Leader." A great majority of the issues I see people having with their dogs stem from a lack of strong pack leadership from the humans involved. As we have learned, dogs are social pack animals with a leader and followers. In the wild, most dogs are followers, but if they don't have a leader to follow, then a dog will attempt to take control of the situation. In a human household, this can cause the dog to show all kinds of unwanted behaviors, including anxiety, destructiveness, excessive barking, and aggression. Not having a strong leader leaves a dog in an unbalanced mental state, and she will then do what she thinks she has to in order to fulfill her needs.

For comparison, imagine this scenario: You are abruptly taken from your home and brought to the Oval Office. A Secret Service agent tells you, "You're the President now. Good luck," and then leaves, offering no further instructions. Only a rare person wouldn't make terrible mistakes in a day or two. A dog without strong leadership is stuck in the same situation.

That strong leadership is often not there because people, especially in the United States, have a tendency to love and pamper

Puppies first experience calm, assertive energy with their mothers.

their dogs, and they think of any kind of discipline or correction as being "mean." Instead of providing direction and protection, which is the Pack Leader's job, many people try to reason with their dogs, like they would with a five-year-old child.

The only problem is that you cannot explain things to a dog in intellectual terms because dogs are instinctual beings. Your dog will just meet you with a puzzled look when you say, "Bella, it makes Mommy really upset when you chew on her nice things, so please don't do it anymore." The dog has no idea what Mommy is talking about. A canine mother would be silent and direct, using her energy, eye contact, and touch to get the message—"Stop"—across to her errant puppy.

The Pack Leader also doesn't communicate with emotional or nervous energy, but is always calm and assertive, using that energy to influence the behavior of the pack. Now, you may be wondering exactly how you project calm and assertive energy. One thing I frequently tell people is to imagine someone they look up to—a favorite teacher, a historical figure, a fictional hero—and then to carry themselves as if they are that person. This mental image will influence your body language, and project that calm, assertive energy. It's hard to slouch when you're imagining yourself as Cleopatra or King Arthur. If you think this idea sounds silly, look at a calm, confident dog sometime, and notice how he moves—proudly, with head and ears up, and always with intention.

It is also very important as the Pack Leader that you claim ownership of your territory, which you can do by asserting yourself in a calm, confident way. This makes it clear to your dog that you own the space in which she lives, and will help her to respect your authority. Along with claiming ownership, you must teach your dog to work for food and affection by taking her for a walk before you feed her. In addition to making your dog work physically, you should also make her work psychologically by having her wait until she is in a calm, submissive state before providing food or affection.

Most important, as a leader, you must know your pack and what their needs are, then help fulfill those needs by creating a structured, consistent environment with Rules, Boundaries, and Limitations. *Dominance* is not a dirty word. In fact, because most dogs do not want to be leaders, your dog will appreciate you all the more for taking control.

The Core Principles in this chapter cover a lot of different areas. There are principles that center squarely on your state of mind, your energy, and your intention. Others rely upon your recognition of intrinsic truths about your dog and how he experiences the world. Putting these ideas together lays a powerful foundation upon which we can build a framework for our dogs and our lives together. The next chapter takes us through practical, simple, and powerful techniques that, again, I rely upon to create balance and happiness in my dogs.

CHAPTER FOUR

Practical Techniques for Every Pack Leader

The journey to transforming yourself into a strong Pack Leader is different for everyone. For some, it might be a long trip, while it may feel like a walk around the block for others. Either way, it all begins with one simple step: seeing your dog for what she really is. And the best way to do that is by relying on your knowledge of the Natural Dog Laws and the Core Principles. Next, let's put these into action with some practical techniques.

Knowledge is just one part of the equation in creating balance in your life. It's wonderful to be armed with information, but you have to use those lessons to set up the proper framework for you and your dog. The five Pack Leader Techniques described in this chapter are all based on a solid foundation of the Natural Dog Laws and Core Principles. Don't be deceived by the simplicity of these techniques—they are powerful tools, and their use will result in a much more rewarding relationship between you and your dog.

PACK LEADER TECHNIQUE #1:
Project Calm, Assertive Energy.

Because energy is so important in the dog world, humans have to know and understand what kind of energy to project to have a happy, healthy dog. Projecting calm, assertive energy is one of the essential parts of being a Pack Leader. If you're looking for a great role model for calm, assertive energy, think of Oprah Winfrey or the Olympic swimmer Michael Phelps. Their strong leadership in their respective fields is communicated not only in how they speak but also in how they carry themselves—self-possessed, confident, and in control.

Your dog's energy is different than yours. Your dog should be calm and submissive, the natural state of a "follower" in a dog pack. When a dog embodies this calm, submissive energy, she relaxes her posture, holds her ears back, and responds easily to your commands.

Often, the first energy that a puppy experiences after birth is his mom's calm, assertive energy that gives the pup his first taste of safety and security. Later, the puppy will most likely follow a pack leader who projects the same calm, assertive energy out of association. As pack followers, dogs return a calm, submissive energy that completes the pack balance. It is important to understand that most dogs are born to be submissive, because there can only be so many pack leaders.

When you couple a calm, assertive person with a calm, submissive dog, it creates a natural balance that nurtures stability and creates a balanced, centered, and happy dog. But when a naturally submissive dog lives with a human who does not lead, she will attempt to right the pack balance by filling what she sees as a vacant pack leader role. This is how behavior problems develop.

To establish yourself as the Pack Leader, you must always project a calm, assertive energy. For instance, when dogs come into our homes, many of them are encountering intense human emotional energy for the very first time. We shower them with affection and babble at them in high-pitched baby talk, so they see us as excited energy—not calm and assertive. This is why many dogs don't listen to their human caretakers. Their mothers never acted this way. It's unnatural to them.

For evidence, you need look no further than my partnership with my four-year-old pit bull, Junior. Junior and I have been together since he was a puppy. We spend all of our time together. Junior has more frequent-flier mileage than most people—over 200,000 miles crisscrossing the world helping to educate, rescue, or rehabilitate dogs in need. I rarely have to speak to him, yet he knows what I want him to do. Our communication is almost all nonverbal. When I am in a large city like New York, I will take Junior for a nighttime walk off leash. Junior stays right by my side, and people are amazed at how "in tune" Junior is to me. There is probably no other city in the world that is more distracting than Manhattan, but during our nightly walks, Junior stays right by my side, reading my every move.

Last summer, Junior and I went to New York City for a press trip. During the trip, I received a frantic call from a very wealthy client who had a problem with her Airedale terrier, named Paris. Her owner had decided to throw a big tenth birthday party for Paris in the posh Hamptons. It was going to be one of the biggest social parties of the summer season. The only problem was that Paris had become fearful and refused to come out from under the dining room table. This went on for two days, and the problem persisted until the day before the party. The owner was desperate, so Junior and I stopped over to help.

Paris's energy was that of severe fear, which was resulting in aggression. I led Junior into the house, and he sensed the potential danger. I just stood back; Junior knew what I wanted him to do. After 15 minutes with Paris under the table, he was able to bring Paris out where I could work with her to relieve her anxiety and fear. Needless to say, Junior was invited to the birthday party the next day.

Without having the luxury of language, dogs have to rely on their advanced intuition, senses, and instincts. And we humans need to learn to recognize them. When we do that, we can achieve amazing results.

▶ TECHNIQUES IN ACTION:
How to Change Your Energy

As I've said, your energy will determine how your dog sees you in your role as Pack Leader. All your energy—good and bad—is a reflection of your state of body, mind, and intention. Calm, assertive energy, for instance, reveals itself with a confident demeanor, straight shoulders, a deliberate gait, and the clear-sightedness that comes from knowing exactly what you want from this moment. The following exercise will help you identify your current energy and the energy of those around you by focusing on two opposing states: positive and negative.

IDENTIFYING POSITIVE ENERGY

It helps to have a partner or a mirror for this exercise:

1. Standing in front of a trusted friend (or mirror), think about a time when you have felt truly positive about life. Picture yourself at a happy, expansive moment and channel that energy. Close your eyes if it helps. For a minute or two, do your best to put yourself back in that positive state of mind.

2. Adjust your body to match the positive state in your head. Notice what's happening to your arms, chest, shoulders, and facial expression. How are you breathing?

3. If you're with someone, ask that person to mirror any changes he or she notices. Like I've said, energy is contagious and influences those around you. Ask that person to demonstrate to you the way your body changed as you filled yourself with positive thoughts.

4. Being aware of your energy is the first step toward changing it. In the hours or days after this exercise, try to replicate the positive energy state you created. Even if you are not feeling good, adjusting your body and mind in a positive direction can have a powerful impact on the energy you convey to the world and to your dog.

IDENTIFYING NEGATIVE ENERGY
Do this exercise with a partner or in front of a mirror:

1 Picture yourself at a time when you were feeling down, angry, or frustrated. For a minute or two, put yourself in that negative state of mind.

2 Adjust your body to match the negative state of mind. Notice what's happening to your arms, chest, shoulders, and facial expression. How has your breathing changed?

3 If you're with someone, ask that person to mirror any changes he or she notices in your body language. Negative energy is just as contagious as positive energy and influences those around you. Ask that person to show you the way your body and energy changed as you filled your head with negative thoughts and fear or anxiety.

4 Take a deep breath and return to the positive state from the first part of the exercise. For a minute or two, bring your mind back to that happy, powerful, inspired state. Notice how much control you have over your positive and negative states of mind.

You may try repeating these exercises with your dog near you to see what kind of reaction occurs with your dog. How does he act when your energy changes? You can also practice with your children or a spouse. Once you understand how you are directly affecting others, you will become more conscious of your own energy and how it can influence your dog and others.

PACK LEADER TECHNIQUE #2:
Give Exercise, Discipline, and Affection—in That Order.

If you're at all familiar with my work, then you know my "fulfillment formula" for dogs: "Exercise, Discipline, and then Affection . . . in that order." Unfortunately, people in many places give their dogs affection, affection, and affection. The end result of this is an unbalanced dog.

I hear a lot of excuses from people who don't provide their dogs enough exercise through the walk: "I don't have time to walk the dog every day"; "My dog plays in the yard all day long, so he doesn't need a walk"; "I have mobility issues and cannot walk my dog"; and so on, and so forth. The truth is: If you take responsibility by adopting a dog, then you must accept responsibility for all aspects of her life, and exercise is one of them.

If you don't have time, then make the time. If you physically cannot walk your dog yourself, then hire a professional dog walker or, at the least, invest in a treadmill. Even if your dog has a yard, he still needs to be walked—running around the yard all day is not the proper type of exercise, as it is not focused and it is not natural for a dog to remain trapped in one location. Remember, the walk is not about the dog going to the bathroom; the walk isn't over just because your dog has done her business.

The purpose of exercising your dog through the walk is twofold. First, it drains your dog's excess energy in a natural, focused way. When a dog is walking and moving forward, his mind is also directed forward, as it would be in natural pack migration to hunt for food. This provides mental stimulation, as well as work for the dog to do before receiving food. Another purpose of the walk is to bond with your dog, and I will have more on this subject later in this chapter.

The second part of the formula, discipline, is intimidating to some people, probably because the word can have negative connotations. A lot of people interpret *discipline* to mean "punishment," but it does not mean this. A better definition is training to act in accordance with the rules. A "well-disciplined army" does not mean a bunch of soldiers who have been whipped; it means a group of people who work well together because they follow the same rules. That is the goal with the discipline part of the formula, to ensure that you and your dog work well together under the rules.

The most important thing to teach your dog is to enter a calm, submissive state when you request it, and the quickest way to ensure this behavior is, of course, to drain your dog's energy through exercise. This is why discipline is the second part of the formula. Once your dog is tired, her mind will turn toward rest, and moving her into calm submission will be much easier. It is also essential that your dog is in a calm, submissive state before moving on to the last part of the formula.

After your dog has been exercised, has followed your requests, and is in a calm, submissive state, only then is it time to give affection. This is an ideal time to feed your dog, because she has worked for it on the walk and by following the rules. You can also offer treats, or petting, but you should stop immediately if your dog moves out of the calm, submissive state. If you offer playtime as a reward, then stop if your dog starts to become aggressive or overly excited.

Although I constantly have to teach people about exercise and discipline, I rarely have to explain how to give affection. That's why it is so important to learn this technique and repeat it to yourself: "Exercise, Discipline, and then Affection . . . in that order."

PACK LEADER TECHNIQUE #3:
Establish Rules, Boundaries, and Limitations — and Enforce Them.

So you're living in the moment, projecting calm, assertive energy, and working with Mother Nature by remembering the five Natural Dog Laws and following the Core Principles. You're practicing Exercise, Discipline, and Affection. Now what? To completely establish your status as the Pack Leader, you need to give your dog Rules, Boundaries, and Limitations, and then enforce them consistently so you do not confuse your dog. This structure plus consistency will do wonders for your dog's state of mind.

In the natural pack, a puppy's mother begins doing this from the very beginning, using touch and scent to control where the puppy goes, when he plays, and when he eats. If the puppy is misbehaving, the mother will gently take the puppy's head in her mouth as a correction, and she will pick the pup up by the scruff and carry him back to the den if he wanders too far. A balanced mother dog is never emotional or excited when dealing with her puppies.

Adult dogs also need to know what they can and cannot do, and as their Pack Leader, you need to teach them. At the very least, you should teach your dog the basic commands of "sit," "stay," "drop it," "come," "down," and "heel." When training, begin by using your energy and gestures rather than words. "Sit" is a perfect command to begin with, because you'd be surprised how many dogs naturally sit when you approach them with calm, assertive energy and lean in slightly toward them.

When a dog has performed the desired command, reward her with a treat, praise, or whatever motivates that particular dog. As you repeat the training and the dog becomes better at complying with the command immediately, you can begin to add the spoken command if you'd like. Keep in mind, though, that it doesn't matter what words you use. A dog can just as easily learn to sit at the sound of the word *pencil*.

During training, if your dog begins to show signs of distraction by glancing around, yawning, or becoming hyperactive, then it is time to stop for a while. Puppies have a lower endurance than adult dogs and will become bored or distracted more quickly.

"Sit" and "stay" are essential commands for teaching your dog boundaries—or, in other words, claiming your space and defining their territory. If you don't want your dog to go into a certain room, have her sit and stay outside the doorway as you go into the room, and correct her if she tries to enter the room, using your body language to make her step back. Be consistent. If you don't want the dog ever to enter that room, then you can never let her enter. If she can enter sometimes, then it can only be upon your invitation.

Whenever leaving the house, you must be the first one to walk out the door as well as the first one to walk in the door upon returning. Again, use "sit" and "stay" to get your dog to wait quietly while you go first, then invite her to follow. This will help teach your dog that you own the space, and reinforce the idea that you make the rules. It also teaches your dog to wait for you before receiving a desired outcome, emphasizing the source of that outcome—her Pack Leader.

Remember, most dogs are not natural-born leaders, and they do not want to be. However, if they are not given any direction, then they will try to do whatever they can to restore balance to the pack. Unfortunately, a dog in such a state frequently acts out of frustration and anxiety, and so will act out with unwanted and frequently destructive or aggressive behaviors. Most dogs do not know what they are supposed to be doing. They need to be told. By providing strong leadership through creating Rules, Boundaries, and Limitations, you give your dog the gift of direction. She will thank you for it by being calm and submissive, and looking to you as the leader of the pack.

PACK LEADER TECHNIQUE #4: **Master the Walk.**

The single most important activity you can take part in with your dog is the walk. It provides exercise and mental stimulation for your dog and affirms your position as the Pack Leader. In addition to maintaining calm, assertive energy, you should always use a short leash, with the collar located at the top of your dog's neck. This allows you to give corrections with a

The walk is an important daily ritual for Junior and me.

quick tug to the side, which will redirect your dog's attention.

On the walk, your dog should always be next to or behind you. If your dog is in front of you, then she is being the Pack Leader, not you. There are several ways to train your dog to stay in the proper position. One is not to allow your dog to move forward if she gets in front of you. Give a correction and stop, or change direction, and continue to do so until your dog walks behind you. You can also use a walking stick or cane, and hold it in front of your dog to keep her in place.

Mornings are an ideal time for the walk, because your dog will have woken up with full energy, but it is essential that you allow enough time for the walk—at least 30 minutes to an hour—to properly drain your dog's energy. This time may vary, depending upon your dog's age and needs. Senior dogs may be tired out after 15 minutes, while young and energetic dogs may take 90 minutes or more. If your dog has any medical conditions, consult your veterinarian to determine safe limits.

Remember also that the walk is not about your dog sniffing around or relieving herself. To maintain control, keep moving forward for at least the first 15 minutes, and then reward your dog by allowing her to explore or go to the bathroom. Keep this reward time shorter than the walk time, however, and continue the pattern for the duration of the walk.

Don't forget to continue your leadership when you return home. Enter the house first, then invite your dog to follow, and make her wait as you remove and put away her leash. This is an ideal time for feeding, because your dog has just worked for a meal.

Taking the time to walk your dog is the single best method to give her exercise and help her maintain balance. It is also the best method for asserting your pack leadership in a positive way. You should go on the walk at least twice a day, allowing enough time each walk to drain your dog's energy and to maintain her calm, submissive state.

With the walk, you can practice all of my methods for maintaining a balanced dog at the same time. It provides exercise and discipline, with opportunities for some affection. It helps you to establish Rules, Boundaries, and Limitations, and can put you and your dog in touch with nature. Finally, it's a great opportunity for you to learn to live in the moment and adjust your own energy. When you begin to put it all together, you will find that the walk is the most rewarding and productive time in your relationship with your dog, and you will both be better for it.

PACK LEADER TECHNIQUE #5:
Read Your Dog's Body Language.

Energy is the unspoken language of communication, and one of the primary ways dogs use energy to communicate is through their body language. Dogs instinctively understand each other's body language. At the same time, they interpret our body language in their way. If we do not take the time to understand how dogs use body language, then we risk miscommunication.

To start, think of two good (human) friends meeting after a long separation. As soon as they see each other, they may both perk up—standing taller, showing their teeth in broad smiles, walking a little bit faster. They may raise their arms and wave enthusiastically. As they approach, they may trot or even run, and they will come to each other head-on, probably greeting in a tight hug, or at the very least with a vigorous handshake.

Remember—humans perceive the world by sight and touch first, while sight is secondary to dogs and touch comes last (see Chapter 2, page 44). So, for humans, this kind of face-to-face, direct contact upon greeting is quite normal. In the human world, it would be considered very rude to not look at people when meeting them, and making eye contact is seen as showing interest or attention, and rarely as a threat. Even when human strangers meet, they begin by facing each other, making eye contact, and vocalizing—speaking in greeting.

If two strange dogs met this way, it would probably lead to a fight. Everything in their body language in this encounter—approaching face-to-face, making eye contact, vocalizing at each other—indicates aggression. Even two familiar dogs can resort to instinct and snap if either perceives the other as approaching aggressively.

Dogs get to know each other through their strongest sense: smell.

How Dogs Greet Each Other

So the next time you're at the dog park, take a close look at how two dogs approach each other when they meet. If the meeting is friendly, they will use their primary sense—smell—to "say" hello. They will approach each other indirectly and sniff toward the side or rear until they are sure of each other's energy. Observe their general posture and energy, and how they hold their heads, ears, and tails. Dogs express their body language primarily through these body parts, and generally, the height of each corresponds to their level of assertiveness, aggression, or dominance.

Of course, you need to be aware of the physical specifics of your dog. In some breeds, the ears almost always stand up straight;

A calm, submissive dog is often seen sitting or lying down.

in others, they are always floppy. If you pay careful attention, though, you'll be able to tell when your dog's ears are tensed and when they're relaxed. Tension is the same as the ears being held high, and relaxation is the same as them being held low.

It's similar with tails. Some breeds always carry their tail curled over their back, and other breeds are tailless or are (unnecessarily and cruelly) cropped soon after birth. In either case it's hard to tell if the tail is in a high, middle, or low position, unless you practice being able to read its subtle movements.

Now, let's look at some examples of how head, ears, and tail project a dog's body language.

CALM, ASSERTIVE

When a dog is calm and assertive, her head, ears, and tail will be held up, but there will be a lack of tension in the body. If she wags her tail, it will be slow to moderate in speed, and rhythmic. A dog in this state will be deliberate in her movements, either remaining still without pacing, or moving forward with purpose. Remember, though, because very few dogs are born to lead, you will meet very few dogs in this energy state.

CALM, SUBMISSIVE
When a dog is calm and submissive, her ears will lie back against her head and the tail will droop to the middle position. Her body will appear relaxed. A calm, submissive dog will also frequently sit or lie down, with the most submissive dog placing her chin on her paws or the floor. A submissive dog may begin wagging her tail when you make eye contact.

AGGRESSIVE
An aggressive dog shows all the signs of a calm, assertive dog, except that her body will be very tense and tight, almost as if she were leaning forward against a physical restraint. An aggressive dog will also maintain eye contact.

Some aggressive dogs show the more obvious signs of growling, baring their teeth, or barking, but do not let the absence of these things lead you to believe that the dog won't snap or bite. If the body language is tight and tense, leave the dog alone. If the tail is wagging, don't assume this means the dog is friendly. Aggressive dogs will often raise their tail very high and wag it very fast.

FEAR AND ANXIETY
A fearful dog, if he doesn't run away, will try to become smaller. He does this by lowering his head and ears, slouching his body, and bending his legs. A fearful dog will usually hold his tail at the

lowest position, often between the back legs (that's where the expression "running away with his tail between his legs" comes from). As with an aggressive dog, the tail may also wag rapidly, but while in this lowered position.

In some breeds, a fearful dog may raise his hackles, a wide ridge of fur down the center of the back that stands on end. This was originally intended to make the dog look bigger and scare off predators. In some cases, a fearful dog may squint, to protect his eyes. This action may even extend to the upper lip curling to expose the teeth. However, as with an aggressive dog's fast wagging tail, this sign does not mean what it might appear to. In the case of a fearful dog, the teeth baring is a sign of submission and the result of the dog's entire face scrunching up.

"LEAVE ME ALONE"

Regardless of their current energy or mood, some dogs just don't want to be approached by a human at times, and they will let you know. Most frequently, a dog will just turn around and walk away from you. If a dog does this, do not follow after it. Remember: Followers come to their leader. If you follow the dog, then you are not being the Pack Leader. You are also not respecting its wishes.

Other ways a dog will let you know she is not interested is in avoiding eye contact, by turning her head to the side. She may also raise her tail but be inconsistent with the position of her head and ears, due to uncertainty.

A dog that does not want to be approached may also remain very still and stiff, as if by not moving she will become invisible to you. At the most extreme levels of warning, a dog may smack her lips or growl to send the message, "Leave me alone."

By learning to read dogs' body language, you will improve your ability to communicate with them by understanding what they are telling you, as well as being better able to use your calm, assertive energy to redirect their instincts and get the behavior you want.

▶ A Complete Set of Tools

All of these techniques—plus the laws and principles from earlier chapters—are at the heart of my work with dogs. Establish this framework and stick to it. Both you and your dog will benefit from a consistent routine and approach. You'll be fulfilling your role as the Pack Leader, and your dog will embrace a calm, submissive state that comes along with that.

CHAPTER FIVE

Ain't Misbehavin'

Typically, misbehaviors in dogs manifest themselves in one of two ways: Either they appear suddenly, or they are bad habits. If your dog has always had behavior issues, first begin to address the problem by looking at yourself. How are you not fulfilling your dog's needs, or failing to provide necessary pack leadership? We will be dealing with those questions—and solutions—in this chapter.

If your dog's behavior changes abruptly, then your dog is trying to tell you something, and you will need to address the problem by looking at your dog. As you figure out the message your dog is trying to send, you will be able to figure out what is necessary to solve the problem. Has the problem happened more than once? Are any patterns emerging? Does the issue seem out of character for your dog?

For example, if your dog never does her business inside the house but you come home one day to a gift on the carpet, it may not be a cause for concern. Ask yourself whether you missed a regular walk that day or changed something in your dog's diet recently. If the incident does not occur again without a clear cause like those mentioned, then you probably don't have a problem. If it suddenly starts happening multiple times a week, then it's time to get to work fixing it.

In these cases, first rule out any medical explanations. For example, a housebroken dog that suddenly starts regularly urinating in the house may have a bladder infection. Sudden aggression, growling, or shying away from touch may indicate that your dog is in physical pain. If your dog's eating or drinking habits suddenly change—for example, she is eating less or drinking more—then go to the veterinarian first to get a checkup.

If your dog is in good health, then ask yourself, "Has anything in our lives changed recently?" Dogs are very sensitive to change. They can become insecure if they feel confused or threatened. Even something as simple as a change in your daily schedule— like leaving home 30 minutes earlier or later in the morning— can throw off your dog until he gets used to a new routine. The good news is that if you are fulfilling your dog's needs otherwise, with Exercise, Discipline, and Affection (see Chapter 4, page 81), and by providing pack leadership, then she should adapt to any changes rather quickly.

For each misbehavior in this chapter, I describe the problem at hand, talk about its potential causes, and then offer solutions to help bring balance back to your dog.

One final note before we begin. If your dog's behavior—whether habitual or sudden—is causing serious disruption in your pack, you may want to consider calling in a professional trainer or dog behaviorist. Their knowledge and skills will help you understand the problem and come up with a plan to address the behavior. And I must stress that if your dog is showing aggression without a physical cause, food aggression toward any human members of the pack, or has bitten or tried to bite anyone, then call in a professional immediately.

MISBEHAVIOR #1:
Overexcitement

We've all seen overexcited dogs. They're the ones that start jumping or spinning when their people come home. They jump on guests and run all over the house. They pull ahead on the walk, puffing and panting, eager to get to the next thing to smell. They tear around the dog park like they're greyhounds on a racetrack. These dogs are the very definition of "hyperactive."

A dog exhibiting such excitement is not in control, which can be dangerous to both the dog and humans. A jumping dog can slip on the floor and injure his legs or back. His claws can scratch people. If the dog is big enough, he can knock furniture around or knock people down. As the Pack Leader, you should fill your dog with confidence and calm, submissive energy when you return home. Your dog may not look as happy, but trust me—a dog that sits quietly and looks at you when you come home is much, much happier than a dog that is bouncing off the walls.

OVEREXCITEMENT: THE CAUSES
This kind of misbehavior is caused by a combination of excess energy and misdirected affection. An overly excited dog is generally not getting enough exercise, of course. But I frequently find in these cases that not only have the dog's people not done anything to curtail the unwanted behavior in the first place, but they have managed to do the opposite by unknowingly encouraging it.

It is a natural tendency of humans to ascribe our own emotions to dogs, and so our first thought upon seeing our dog jumping up and down upon our return home is that he is very happy to see us. And why wouldn't we think that? Happy humans jump up and down when they've been picked on a game show or their team has scored the winning goal. Humans also jump up and down when they dance, and humans generally dance only when they're happy.

So we come home and our dog greets us by jumping up and down or spinning, and our natural reaction is to be happy too, and to greet the dog with assurances that we missed her just as much. What we are really doing in such a case is giving affection and attention to an unstable dog, and the dog gets only one message: "I like it when you act this way!"

OVERCOMING OVEREXCITEMENT

The first step in dealing with the problem is to ignore your dog when he is exhibiting unwanted behavior. When you come home, if your dog starts jumping or spinning, practice my technique of "No Touch, No Talk, No Eye Contact" (see Chapter 2, page 45). Do not acknowledge your dog while he is overexcited. Instead, go about your normal routine of coming home. Put down whatever you're carrying, take care of whatever business you usually would, and wait until your dog relaxes (by wearing himself out) before saying hello and giving affection.

This method is also necessary if your dog jumps on guests, but you will need to train your visitors as well. Visiting dog lovers tend to have the habit of putting up with excited behavior and giving affection, probably out of fear of appearing rude. As the host, you can educate your guests by asking them to ignore your dog while she is excited. Assure them that neither you nor the dog will take it personally, but that they are helping you to train your dog.

Upon returning home, in general, is also a good opportunity to check your own energy. Your dog is your mirror. Do you tend to be easily excitable or generally boisterous? If you are constantly exhibiting overexcitement, then your dog will reflect this. Talking loudly, dashing around the place, getting upset at little things—all of these will tell your dog that this is how this pack behaves.

Of course, you should burn up your dog's excess energy by taking him on a long, vigorous walk. This is a healthy way to focus all of that energy on moving forward with you, and then using it up. If your dog is hyperactive on the walk, giving him a job by putting a backpack on him will help to wear him out more quickly; the weight of the pack will also focus his attention on carrying it.

One other thing to try to calm an overexcited dog is to appeal to her strongest scent organ, her nose. Some scents, like lavender, are soothing to humans. Dogs are the same, except with much more powerful noses. Consult your veterinarian to find out what smells may work for your dog and which dispersal methods are the safest for her.

Although overexcitement may seem like a relatively harmless problem, in the long run, it is better to teach your dog how to greet you with calm, submissive energy, and it is healthier to allow your dog to use up that excess energy in a positive and focused manner. A jumping, spinning, running dog may appear happy, but that's a human perception. A calm and balanced dog is far happier.

MISBEHAVIOR #2:
Aggression

Aggression in dogs is probably one of the most common issues I am asked to address. Aggression takes many forms. Some dogs are aggressive only toward other dogs or animals; some, only toward people; still others show aggression only around food or high-value treats and toys.

Aggression in dogs is a very noticeable and identifiable behavior, particularly for those on the receiving end. The body language of such dogs is tense and focused, and they often make noise: Aggressive dogs will growl, bark, snarl, bare their teeth, and frequently snap or bite at any person or animal that comes within range. Frequently while being walked, aggressive dogs are difficult to control, pulling at the lead, barking at every other dog or human that they see.

This issue can be one of the most difficult to resolve, particularly in the case of biters, or dogs that are in the "red zone"—that is, dogs that go into attack mode and cannot be brought out of it. In nature, when dogs show aggression, they show it only until they have won the "argument." A red-zone dog, though, is out to kill, and will not stop until he has succeeded.

People with an aggressive dog in the household naturally feel constantly nervous, but this can only make the problem worse. Anxiety, nervousness, and uncertainty are all weak forms of energy, and these states of being just serve to remind the dog that there is no strong Pack Leader around. If any member of your household is feeling fearful because of your dog's aggression, then it is time to call in a professional immediately. Dogs can sense fear in humans and other animals, and an aggressive

Because they often pull and lunge, aggressive dogs can be difficult to control.

dog will take advantage of this weak energy state. Also, if your dog is showing food aggression with any member of the human pack, call a professional.

AGGRESSION: THE CAUSES

Aggression is often caused by a combination of frustration and dominance. The dog may feel frustration because of a lack of exercise, and so is full of pent-up energy. The dog becomes dominant because of a lack of leadership from the humans around him. Combined frustration and dominance cause a dog to lash out and try to take control. Without Rules, Boundaries, and Limitations, a dog has no idea what he is supposed to do (see Chapter 4, page 83). This can be a very confusing and frightening thing for a dog, especially if the dog would not normally assume a leadership position in the pack—and, as I have said before, the large majority of dogs are not natural pack leaders. They are perfectly happy being followers.

The effect of an unrehabilitated aggressive dog on its people and household can be devastating. I have met families who have practically become hermits in their own homes, never allowing any visitors, or never letting their children's friends come over to play. In multiple-pet households, everyone has to play the game of "keep the animals apart," with the aggressive dog shunted from one place to another and kept behind closed doors. With the problem left untreated, someone is inevitably bitten, which escalates the fearfulness and frustration of the people and makes the dog exert further dominance. After a second bite, the humans in the household far too often feel they have only two choices: get the dog out or put the dog down. So for me, solving an aggression problem is one of my most important challenges, because it keeps dogs in homes and it keeps people safe.

Overcoming Aggression

The root causes of most aggression are the same, and so are the solutions. To deal with a dog's aggression, all humans in the household have to establish themselves as the Pack Leader, and the dog needs to be given consistent Rules, Boundaries, and Limitations. During the process, consider your dog in the same way you would a human in rehab—the dog has an issue to deal with, and until he has dealt with it, he does not get to have the same privileges or freedoms that a nonaggressive dog would. This is not punishment. This is structure, and it will simplify your dog's life during the rehabilitation. In particular, be very careful about giving affection. You should do so only when your

Teddy

I have dealt with many aggressive dogs, and Teddy, a nine-year-old yellow Lab mix, was a typical case. His caregivers, Steve and Lisa Garelick, adopted Teddy as a puppy. He naturally had high energy and was aggressive, but because the Garelicks did not provide strong pack leadership from the beginning, Teddy's aggression continued unchecked, directed toward people and other animals.

They tolerated his aggression for nine years. However, with the birth of their daughter, Sara (who was two and a half at the time I visited), they became increasingly concerned. The last thing they wanted was for Teddy to bite Sara. Interestingly enough, though, Sara was the one person toward whom Teddy showed no aggression. This was because the Garelicks did the right thing before she was born: They prepared Teddy for a new arrival in the house, and then made it clear to the dog that this new human had a higher status. They managed to make their daughter Teddy's Pack Leader without knowing it, and yet could not do the same thing for themselves.

The Garelicks did what many people do when their dog shows aggression—they avoided situations that could cause aggression, instead of dealing with the problem. They were afraid that they would not be able to control their dog in those situations. When I showed them that I could control Teddy's aggression by redirecting him out of that state as it was happening, they realized that it was possible. Once I showed them they could do it themselves, their nervousness and anxiety lessened, their confidence increased, and they were on their way to being successful Pack Leaders. ▪

dog is in a calm, submissive state. *Never* show affection when your dog is exhibiting the unwanted behavior, particularly aggression—this just teaches your dog that she can use aggression to get affection.

Establish rules and boundaries. If your dog normally spends her time on the sofa, make it off-limits, for now, and make sure that the dog stays down. Don't worry that your dog will feel insulted by this. Dogs don't think that way. In fact, dealing with the new rule will probably be harder for the humans. When people move around the house, make sure that the dog is never the first one to go through a door into another room; the dog must wait and go after the humans. If your dog does try to lead you, turn around at the door and walk the other way. If you have enough rooms at home to do so, establish one as temporarily off-limits to the dog, with all the humans in the pack consistently not allowing the dog into that room.

Also during the rehabilitation, pick up and put away all of the toys, bones, and other dog playthings around the house, with the goal being to teach your dog that these all belong to you and can be played with only on your terms. Oftentimes, a dog will believe that he is powerful if he gathers a large collection of things, so having all these items lying around for an aggressive dog to hoard can make the issue worse.

Do not let your dog give you commands. Dogs will often try to get our attention by nudging us, putting their heads on our laps, or jumping up. When your dog does this, ignore her; do not even say, "No." Just don't acknowledge the behavior. Otherwise, your dog has just told you what to do, and you did it.

During this entire process, of course, the most important thing you can do is keep your dog well exercised, ideally with long walks. Remember, part of the cause of aggression is excess energy, and you need to drain that energy. If just walking doesn't seem to be enough for your dog, have her wear a backpack to give her a job and help drain energy, or have her tow you on in-line skates or run alongside you while you ride a bicycle. (You should consult a trainer, however, to teach you and your dog how to do this safely.)

The other important aspect of the walk, particularly when it comes to aggression, is pack bonding and establishing leadership. In the wild, dog packs migrate together—in search of food and water, and to explore and establish their territory. The farther they travel, the more likely they are to find a lot of food and water, and the larger their territory becomes. When you exhibit calm, assertive energy and take the lead on the walk, you provide the pack leadership and direction that an aggressive dog needs. Through using a leash, you also have the ideal opportunity to correct unwanted behaviors just before they happen.

As pack animals, dogs are mainly concerned with the entire pack running smoothly, and most dogs would rather be followers than leaders. Aggression within the pack is unnatural, and more dominant members quickly put an aggressive dog in his place. Too often, when we bring dogs into our human packs, we forget to fulfill their needs by being the leaders, and instead indulge them as children, giving them too much unearned affection. With no strong leadership, dogs are thrust into a role they neither want nor can handle, so they lash out at everything because of their frustration. However, aggression is usually not an unsolvable issue, and your dog will thank you with her own loyalty and affection once you restore her proper place in the pack.

MISBEHAVIOR #3:
Anxiety

In the animal world, there are two natural reactions to a threatening stimulus: fight or flight. We saw "fight" in aggression, but not all dogs react this way. It's perfectly natural for a dog to fear something threatening to them, but unnatural anxiety occurs when dogs show extreme fear toward things that cannot hurt them. Fearful dogs may exhibit a range of behaviors, from running off and hiding at the first sudden stimulus to staying in place and quaking in terror. It isn't uncommon for such dogs to suddenly exhibit submissive urination or defecation, so it can be an unpleasant situation for the humans as well. Such dogs can become skittish about everything, from falling objects to people moving to reflections in their water bowl.

Many dogs are fearful, and their first instinct is to run away and hide from anything new. At an extreme, the running away becomes entirely psychological. Ever hear the expression "paralyzed with fear"? This happens when animals become so frightened by something that they lose any ability to control their body and run away in self-preservation. The mind runs away first. In the wild, such fearful animals usually become some other animal's lunch rather quickly.

Don't assume that a fearful dog cannot be dangerous, though. Any animals that feel sufficiently threatened, even if seemingly paralyzed with fear, can still lash out and attack with everything they've got in a last-ditch effort to survive. If left uncorrected, a dog can become fear-aggressive, which can be a very bad match for those with the human tendency to feel sorry for and try to comfort frightened animals.

It can be difficult, if not impossible, for humans and fearful dogs to have a fulfilling relationship. Trust is at the center of resolving this issue. Everything may seem fine, but then the dog can be set off with one wrong move by a human. Establishing a bond of trust can be extremely hard in such cases. In addition, living in a constant state of anxiety can be unhealthy for the dog, leading to an elevated heart rate, rapid breathing, and a steady flow of adrenaline in the system. We would say that a human exhibiting the same symptoms is "stressed out," and it's no different for a dog. Constant, unrelieved anxiety can be physically dangerous, if not fatal.

ANXIETY: THE CAUSES

Extreme anxiety and fearfulness are usually related to low self-esteem, which, for dogs, means that they are uncertain of their status. This can happen for various reasons. Perhaps they were taken away from their mothers too early, and so did not learn to experience the world first through nose, then eyes, then ears. They also would have missed out on proper socialization through their mother's actions of feeding, cleaning, and correcting. Dogs can also have low self-esteem if they experience abuse or isolation early in life. Because the problem is rooted so deeply and early in the dog's life, cases of anxiety take a lot longer to resolve than other issues, like aggression. I usually see results with an aggressive dog in the first half hour. Cases of anxiety can take months.

OVERCOMING ANXIETY

The best way to deal with a dog's low self-esteem is through the power of the pack—in these cases, the power of the dog pack.

Luna

One of the most anxious and fearful dogs I ever worked with was Luna, a year-and-a-half-old yellow Lab mix. She had been adopted from the Pasadena Humane Society as a puppy by Abel Delgado, who chose her because she reminded him of himself when he was young. He explained to me that he grew up in a large family of Mexican immigrants in Los Angeles, and both of his parents worked all the time, so he was left to take care of his younger siblings, but with the constant worry about what he was doing or was supposed to be doing.

Abel is now a music teacher, conductor, and flutist who works with schoolchildren through his own nonprofit foundation, and he has managed to conquer any anxiety issues he had when young. Luna, on the other hand, was not doing so well. As Abel described it, she was terrified of anything that moved or made a noise—basically anything living. Any objects with wheels—bicycles, skateboards, trucks—would send her into a panic on walks, and her only concern was running away, with no regard for her own safety.

One day on a walk, Luna's collar broke and she took off directly into traffic, where she was grazed by a car and then disappeared on the other side of the street. Luckily, Abel found her, uninjured. But it was clear that Luna's problem demonstrated the most extreme form of this kind of anxiety: Her flight response completely overrode her sense of self-preservation, and she literally fled from one danger right into another. It took two solid months at the Dog Psychology Center, but Luna eventually returned to life with Abel, and now can even go with him to work, to calmly watch him conduct a large and very loud student orchestra. ∎

Structured training with other dogs will help with socialization, and will give an anxious dog examples of how to behave. This means working with a trainer, so you should choose one who will also help you find the right energy in yourself and help you learn how to train yourself as you train your dog.

As an anxious dog's self-esteem starts to improve, you can then begin to expose the dog to different stimuli. A treadmill is ideal for this sort of work. Once the dog is comfortable with walking on a treadmill at a steady pace, you can begin to introduce sounds or objects that trigger her flight response, with the goal being that she does not react to them. The reason this works is because the action of walking on the treadmill engages the dog's brain in moving forward, which is the opposite of the flight response. This conditions the dog to then associate the formerly terrifying stimulus with the action of moving toward it.

Further along in the process, begin exposing the dog to different situations, moving in little steps. If possible, have a friend or trainer with another dog on hand, then walk together in areas with other dogs, then other people; find places with unusual noises or smells; walk near a bike or skate path. With calm, assertive humans and another balanced dog in the mix, the anxious dog will begin to trust himself in such situations. This is also one of the few times when I recommend using a retractable-type lead, although sparingly and with caution—you want to encourage an anxious dog to be able to move away from you to explore, while also coming back to you should he become frightened, or when you call him back.

Anxious dogs frequently do well with agility training, because it gives them a clear set of goals to accomplish. Begin small, with only one or two sets of challenges, and then gradually expand the course. And remember—you're not training the next world champion agility dog here; that isn't the point. You are giving your dog a series of small goals; your dog's confidence will increase with each one successfully reached.

If your dog is not anxious at home, but shows fearful behavior only when outside of the home, then you can try to use the dog's nose to relieve the behavior. Start placing a drop or two of a pleasant scent, like lavender oil, on your hand before events that are pleasurable for your dog, like feeding time. Let the dog explore the scent and get used to it. Then, associate this smell with the experience of going on the walk in the same way, by placing a couple of drops on your hand before you pick up the leash. Once on the walk, if you see a situation coming that would normally make your dog panic, get out the scent (before the panic), and use it to distract your dog's mind through his sense of smell and the pleasant association you have created.

Finally, whenever your dog moves into a fearful state, do not try to make her feel better with affection. Instead, maintain your calm, assertive energy, and practice my technique of "No Touch, No Talk, No Eye Contact." Unlike humans, when dogs receive affection, they interpret it as approval of how they are behaving in that moment, and not as an attempt to make them feel "better." So if you pet your dog and tell him, "It'll be OK," when he is in a fearful mode, what he understands is that you are telling him, "It's OK to be this way. I will give you affection because you are scared." This only reinforces the undesired behavior.

Fear is a powerful emotion in humans and dogs, but dogs do not have the ability to rationalize it away. They have only two instinctive reactions to fear: attack the source or run away from it. In a pack situation, some dogs are protectors. The dogs that aren't protectors do not worry about whether they should be when danger approaches. Outside of the pack, though, dogs can wind up with no idea what their role is supposed to be. When this uncertainty is combined with a threatening stimulus, the dog can panic, and then lose all self-trust in knowing how to act at any given time. Although it is a difficult problem to resolve, even the most timid and anxious dog can be rehabilitated with time, patience, and the right tools.

MISBEHAVIOR #4:
Fear of Loud Noises

Thunder is one of the most awesome sounds in nature. If you've ever been outdoors and away from a big city during a thunderstorm, then you've heard the deep boom that seems to explode from everywhere and rolls past in waves. It's almost a living sound, and can be quite wonderful to listen to if you have no fear of it and understand that it's produced when lightning strikes and heats the air. But to many dogs, this noise is terrifying.

It is not uncommon for dogs to show extreme fear in the presence of loud, unexpected noises. In addition to thunder, fireworks, gunshots, a car backfiring, or any number of abrupt sounds can also cause this reaction. It's no accident that, in the United States, the Fourth of July and its fireworks coincide with the highest number of runaway dogs for the year.

It's not fun to watch an otherwise calm and happy dog turn into a nervous wreck during a sudden storm or because of a festive celebration. Unfortunately, once a dog has reached this state, it can be very difficult to calm him down. As I've mentioned elsewhere, affection will not do anything except reinforce the unstable state. And, unfortunately, although we can predict the Fourth of July, people cannot really predict the weather accurately. If you can—then you can probably get your own TV show as a storm whisperer!

FEAR OF LOUD NOISES: THE CAUSES

Humans know that thunder is a completely natural phenomenon. However, for many animals, dogs included, a loud noise like thunder can induce a primal fear. They do not associate the flash of lightning with the burst of sound. To them, the noise comes from everywhere, so there is nowhere to hide. It also comes from above, which is the direction from which predators generally attack.

OVERCOMING FEAR OF LOUD NOISES

Unlike other issues, dealing with a fear of loud noises can be difficult because the noises are either unpredictable or come only once a year. You can plan ahead for the Fourth of July, however, and it is never too soon to start. Preparing your dog now for future fireworks will prevent a lot of issues, as well as help mitigate problems with other unexpected loud noises.

You can begin at any time by slowly getting your dog used to noises. Download sounds of fireworks, thunder, explosions, and other loud noises, and then start playing them at low volume while your dog is engaged in pleasurable activity, like eating or playing. Slowly increase the volume each day until your dog seems comfortable and undistracted by the sounds.

If an unexpected storm comes up, try distracting your dog during it. Work with her on obedience behaviors, like sitting or shaking, and reward her with treats. Put a backpack on her, or put her on a treadmill. The goal here is to focus your dog's attention on something other than the thunder. You can also use your dog's nose to distract her from the noise by exposing her to pleasant scents, like lavender or pine. If necessary, keep your dog on a leash next to you, even in the house. This will help prevent her from running away and keep her in the presence of your calm, assertive energy.

Remember that you have one advantage as a human—you can use the lightning to tell you when the thunder is coming, and then maintain calm and assertive energy as you wait expectantly for the loud noise, turning it into a game with your dog. Tell her, "Here it comes, here it comes," and then, when the thunder strikes, celebrate with her. This will begin to associate the loud noise with affection, and will demonstrate your lack of fear with your positive energy.

On any day in which you know fireworks are going to occur, take your dog for a long walk well before the celebrations begin, and drain her energy. If you normally walk for a half hour, go for two hours instead. You want your dog to be so exhausted that her brain won't even register the fireworks. You can also consider using dog-safe earplugs to reduce the intensity of the noise, which may be enough to prevent a flight reaction. And, of course, be sure that your dog is always wearing ID and, ideally, has an ID microchip, in case the noise does cause her to run away.

Although loud noises do occur in nature, many dogs are frightened by them and will attempt to flee, if possible. However, by draining your dog's energy with exercise, engaging her attention elsewhere, or slowly getting her used to the sounds, you can go a long way toward minimizing any negative reactions, so that a summer storm or a fireworks show becomes just another noise.

Insecure fences can be irresistible temptations to dogs who like to roam or chase.

 MISBEHAVIOR #5:
Running Away

Some dogs are runners, and will take off at the first chance they get. In some cases, the behavior is opportunistic, and a dog will take advantage of an opened door or unlocked gate to go exploring. Other times, a dog will actively try to escape, burrowing under or leaping over a fence. You've probably even seen similar behavior at an off-leash dog park, with a person frantically chasing after a dog when it's time to go home, and the dog refusing to come, no matter how many times her person calls, turning it into a game of "catch me if you can."

Chula

Chula, a two-year-old Shiba Inu, was a classic example of a runner, and she would bolt out the front door whenever she found it open. This was a great concern to her people, Rita and Jack Stroud, because Chula would just take off, not looking where she was going. If they tried to chase her, she would turn it into a game by running farther away. On the walk, Chula would pull, trying to investigate or chase anything that came across her path. At home, she would jump from one piece of furniture to another, claiming each as her own.

In Chula's case, I soon determined that Rita and Jack were walking her only one day a week, and were not discouraging her from jumping on the furniture. Because the Shiba Inu was bred as a hunting dog specializing in flushing out small prey, Chula's natural instincts were not being fulfilled. The Strouds admitted that they spoiled her; without discipline, Chula was really running the household. Everything inside of the house was her kingdom, and so was everything outside. Once the Strouds established Rules, Boundaries, and Limitations, Chula's behavior inside the house improved and her tendency to run away faded. They can even leave the front door open now, and Chula will stay inside. ∎

It is actually more dangerous for a dog to run away in the human world than it is in the wild. The dog can become lost, or be killed or injured running into the street. The dog may be found by other humans, and without proper identification or a microchip, may never be returned to his original family. Dogs that take every opportunity to run off will probably wind up thinking they are in charge of the pack and will be impossible to control or discipline at home.

Running Away: The Causes

As with many other canine misbehaviors, the root causes of dogs fleeing the den are lack of leadership and mental stimulation, plus excess energy. Unlike humans who leave for work or school and leave the dogs behind, it is very unusual in nature for one or more members of a pack to leave the rest and wander off on their own. There's no reason to. If a dog spots something to chase, it will alert the pack, and they will hunt together.

Although any dog can exhibit runaway behavior, certain breeds—particularly from the working, hound, and hunting groups of dogs—can be more likely to take off, as they follow their inbred instinct to chase prey.

Overcoming Running Away

First, spaying or neutering your dogs will reduce their tendency to wander, especially male dogs. Having your dogs fixed, especially at an early age, will eliminate the hormonal signals that can induce wandering in search of a mate or the desire to claim their own territory. Neutered dogs are also less likely to mark inside the home, become aggressive, or get into fights.

Next, it is necessary to create boundaries, building an invisible barrier in every doorway. To do this, the humans in the household must claim these doorways as their own, training dogs so that they will not pass through without permission.

The beginning of each of several daily walks is the ideal time for this training. First, the dog must be in a calm, submissive state and sit quietly before you even put on the leash. Next, lead the dog to the door and open it, but do not allow the dog to go out. Make the dog sit on the inside of the open door and wait. You go out first. The dog is not allowed to follow you until you give her a clear and definite signal to do so. When returning home, repeat the procedure in reverse. Open the door, but do not allow the dog to enter first. Do this consistently every single time you walk the dog, and always vary the length of time you make the dog wait before going in and out. Especially early on, make the dog wait until she has stopped making any moves in anticipation of going out the door and is focused on you.

On the walk itself, keep the dog close to your side, and use a short lead to keep his head up. Do not allow him to sniff at or investigate anything on the ground for the first part of the walk. You keep moving forward, and the dog moves with you. When you can walk for a while with the dog at your side and not pulling, then you may reward him by allowing him to sniff at the ground briefly, before returning to moving forward with the dog at your side.

You should set boundaries on the walk as well, particularly at corners before crossing streets. Stop at the corner and make the dog stop next to you until she is calm and submissive, sitting if possible. Your dog is not allowed to cross the street until you give her permission; only when you begin to cross the street can she follow next to you. It may take a few tries at first to get your dog to stop and recognize the curb, but if you are consistent and do this at every street crossing, eventually the dog will stop before you tell her to, recognizing the boundary you have defined.

While you are working on creating these boundaries, you should also be working with your dog on "recall," which is a term trainers use for calling your dog to come back to you. This will help reduce a dog's tendency to turn her running away into a game of "catch me if you can." For recall training, you may use a long lead. Move as far as possible away from the dog and call her. If the dog does not return, reel her in, and then move away and repeat the procedure. When she comes to you when called, reward her with affection or a treat.

Eventually, when the boundary of waiting before going out the door is second nature for your dog, work with her on waiting just outside the door. You can use the long lead for this exercise as well. Have your dog sit in a spot by the door, and then move away. If the dog begins to move from the spot, correct her and make her go back to the spot. Continue this for as long as necessary until the dog remains in the spot. Often, when the dog understands what's expected, she will just lie down calmly in the spot.

Reinforce this waiting behavior at every opportunity you have. If you take your dog to a strange place with a door or a gate, then make the dog wait. You should also do the same with the car, letting the dog get in or out only when you give permission.

If you are concerned about your dog running off, then a GPS tracking device is a worthwhile investment. Worn like a collar, these devices include a tracker and wireless link. If your dog moves outside of a designated area, the device activates and will send a signal to your smartphone or computer showing the dog's current location.

As pack animals with a territorial instinct, dogs are not naturally inclined to flee from home. However, without the proper exercise, discipline, mental stimulation, or rules, any dog may run off simply out of boredom, looking for something more interesting somewhere else. If you provide for your dog's needs and make sure he is balanced and fulfilled, then he will have no reason to run off. If you create rules and boundaries regarding going in and out of the house, your dog will be far less inclined to take advantage of an open door.

 Misbehavior #6:
Obsession

Obsession in dogs is different than in humans. We often say that humans are obsessed if they exhibit a strong interest in a hobby, a movie star, or a sports team—except for extreme cases, this sort of human obsession doesn't interfere with day-to-day life. Because dogs do not intellectualize or rationalize their behavior, however, obsession can and usually does interfere with their lives, and with the lives of their owners.

What do we mean by "obsession" in dogs? This is when dogs become fixated on a certain behavior, locked in a mental state that keeps them focused on that one thing. Obsessive behavior can take many forms: chasing shadows, lights, or reflections; running or moving in constant circles; and licking or chewing on themselves without a physical cause such as a skin condition or a cut. When dogs reach this level of obsession, snapping them out of it can be very difficult.

Obsession: The Causes

There are two main causes of obsession in dogs. One is excess energy that the dog needs to release. In this case, the dog will engage in the behavior until he exhausts himself. This type of obsession is usually the easiest to correct. The second and more difficult cause is insecurity. This can develop in a dog because of a trauma or panic-inducing event, particularly if the event occurs when the dog is young. When dogs exhibit insecure, obsessive behavior, they are letting us know that they lack strong leadership and direction, and so are focusing in an unhealthy way on something that makes them feel a false sense of security.

At times, insecurity can lead to excess energy and fuel the cycle of obsession. When a dog is in a state of constant alert, he is producing excess energy, as if he is wired on caffeine—always anxious, always hunting for an object of obsession. So dogs that are obsessed because of insecurity will often also work themselves up into a state of excess energy, and this becomes a feedback loop: Insecurity fuels obsession, which leads to a heightened state of anxiety, which creates excess energy, which fuels the obsession, and so on.

When the weather gets too hot, this cycle can actually be dangerous, leading a dog to overheat. An improper mental state can truly become a physical danger—but the problem can be dealt with.

Overcoming Obsession

To help your dog regain his balance, first you must figure out the cause of his behavior. Is your dog insecure, does he have excess

Brooks

Why does insecurity lead to obsession? Control. Having been frightened by something beyond their control, dogs can become neurotic, searching until they find that one thing they can control or that at least cannot turn around and attack. I dealt with exactly this in the case of Brooks, a five-year-old Entlebucher, or Swiss mountain dog, that would chase any sort of light or reflection, often running into people, furniture, or walls in his obsession.

When I met with Brooks's owners, Lorain and Chuck Nicholson, I quickly determined the cause of the problem. As a puppy, Brooks was frightened first by being introduced too quickly to a neighbor's dog, and then by a car backing out of a driveway. He became timid and fearful—and then Lorain's brother-in-law introduced him to the game of "chase the laser pointer," which Brooks took to, but way too much.

Having been frightened by large things beyond his control, Brooks had discovered something small and harmless. The light lured him into the chase because he learned that he could take control of it and be dominant. When the light wasn't there, he would actively search for it, indulging in the obsession at anything similar, even the glossy shine of a wooden floor. Even on the walk, Brooks was at constant alert, searching the ground for any sign of a light to chase. Brooks responded almost immediately to redirection from his obsession when I began correcting him, and the Nicholsons were able to resolve the problem in a month or two of consistent correction, and by establishing Rules, Boundaries, and Limitations. ▪

energy, or is it a combination of both? Zeroing in on the cause will help you determine the best solution for your pet.

If you believe the cause is excess energy, then make sure that your dog is getting plenty of exercise with long walks, and that you then redirect attention away from any sign of the obsessive behavior toward a desired calm, submissive state of mind. Dogs that constantly dig in their backyards are usually frustrated because they don't get enough exercise. If you have a strong breed that likes to run and can outlast you on a walk, try strapping a backpack on the dog before the walk. Alternatively, your dog can pull you on a bike or in-line skates to help exhaust her before you become too tired. You can also help redirect the obsession by providing mental challenges, like a rubber chew toy with a treat hidden inside.

To rehabilitate an obsessive dog, it is necessary to snap the dog out of the obsessive state of mind as it is about to happen, and the walk is an ideal venue to begin. (If your dog does not exhibit obsessive behavior on the walk, congratulations. You're halfway there.) You'll require a short lead and a correcting collar that sits high up on the neck, such as the Illusion Collar. Use this to give a correction with a short, gentle tug as soon as the dog shows any sign of moving into the obsessive state. If you give the tug too early or too late, the technique will not work. It's all about the right timing.

In obsessions that involve chasing things, your dog will try to investigate the ground with her eyes. Your goal is to keep your dog's head up, eyes ahead, moving forward with you. As soon as your dog tries to lower her head or look around distractedly, give the correction. It's important that you do this the instant you sense your dog starting to move into the undesired mental state, and vital that you are consistent with the correction.

At first, your dog may try to "win" by outlasting you and getting what she wants. Do not give up, and do not give in. Most important, do not feel frustrated if your dog doesn't get it at first. Maintain a calm, assertive energy at all times and remember: Your dog will not feel resentment when you show strong leadership. In fact, an insecure dog will appreciate it, because that is exactly what she needs. Continue with this process on the walk until you no longer need to give the correction to snap your dog out of the obsession.

Meanwhile, you will also need to deal with your dog's obsession at home, and in a similar fashion. With the same lead and collar, take your dog around the house to the places where she engages in her obsessive behavior, again making the correction just as your dog starts to move into the obsessive state. You will need to do this in every room where the dog is allowed, to teach her that she is not to engage in the obsession just because, for example, she's in the kitchen.

Eventually, instead of focusing on the obsession, the dog should begin to focus on you, showing calm, submissive energy. This is when you can offer praise, a treat, or whatever positive reinforcement works for your dog. As Pack Leaders, we have to redirect that energy, and teach our dogs that they do not have to chase reflections or spin in circles for everything to be all right in their world.

MISBEHAVIOR #7:
Hoarding

Some dogs will engage in hoarding behavior, hiding food, toys, or treats by "burying" them in furniture (such as under bedclothes or sofa cushions), or hiding them in corners, closets, or other out-of-the-way places. More than one dog owner has gone to bed only to find a pile of kibble under the pillow, or has swept under the bed only to discover every "lost" dog toy.

Allowing a dog to hoard like this can cause a dog to become possessive or aggressive over hidden food, protecting his stash from anyone who comes near it. It can also be messy and unsanitary, especially if you feed your dog wet or raw food or give him unstripped bones. You can only imagine how unpleasant it can be to have an unidentified smell around the house, only to find months later that it's because of a pile of wet food hidden in a closet. (Well, the smell is unpleasant for humans. Insects and rodents would and do consider it a banquet, which is another reason it is not a good practice to allow.)

Finally, although the inside of a house is not like a forest with soft dirt everywhere, your dog won't necessarily perceive it that way. A sofa cushion can feel like dirt to a dog, and so can a carpet. A dog sees nothing wrong with quickly ripping through upholstery. He doesn't care if it's $3,000 Italian leather or a $300 special from IKEA. In the moment, he's just indulging in a natural instinct to dig and bury. A dog can do some serious damage to a carpet as well, but carpet can also do serious damage to a dog's nose if he tries to root it up.

Hoarding: The Causes

Hoarding has its roots in the behavior of wild dogs, and it is an evolutionary holdover. In the wild, there is no secure source of food. The pack hunts. Sometimes it will find little to no food; sometimes it will hit the jackpot and have an overabundance. It was quite natural, then, for the wild pack to hide extra food to have around for those times when the hunt was not successful, and the most common hiding method was to dig a hole and bury it.

Our modern household dogs generally do not have a problem with an irregular food supply. We are there to give them their kibble or wet food on a more-or-less consistent daily schedule. However, the inbred desire to ensure that there will be food in times of a lean hunt can drive some dogs to store away extra. Especially because there is always an adequate food supply, dogs with this drive may even hide some food before they begin to eat, grabbing a mouthful and running into another room. They don't do this because they don't like being watched when they eat. They do it to protect that imagined surplus.

Overcoming Hoarding

To deal with hoarding behavior for toys, you also must take control of the toys. Similar to part of the process of dealing with aggression, you need to gather up toys your dog is hoarding and put them somewhere out of your dog's reach. Allow your dog to have only one or two toys at a time—she cannot play with more than one at a time anyway. Because she has no extra toys, she will remain focused on the ones in front of her and resist the urge to hide them because she will have no extra toys if she does.

The best way to stop the food-hoarding problem is to take control and structure your dog's mealtime. Always take your dog on a long walk first, which allows her to work for her food. When you return home, prepare the food, and then make your dog sit and wait before you fill her bowl. When she can remain sitting quietly, projecting calm, submissive energy, place the bowl in front of her. When she stops eating and walks away from the bowl, mealtime is done. Remove the bowl and do not feed her again until you have repeated all of these steps.

By removing the food when your dog stops eating, you are also removing the temptation for your dog to come back later and hide the extra. There will always be just enough food, but never so much that there's any to save for a "rainy day."

Hoarding is one of those behaviors where a dog's most ancient instincts collide with the modern world. The ironic result of feeding our dogs so well is that it can trigger in them a famine mentality because dogs live in the moment. They do not remember that you gave them a huge bowl of food yesterday nor do they know you are going to do so tomorrow. Rather, they see a huge bowl of food in front of them now, and an opportunity to not go hungry if they manage to save away what they don't eat. Taking control of the rules of eating will eliminate unwanted hoarding behavior. It will also help to keep your dog from becoming obese. That's two benefits for the price of one solution.

MISBEHAVIOR #8:
Excessive Barking

It's a simple fact of life. Dogs bark. It's one of their forms of communication, with many possible causes and meanings. It can be simply a response to a sudden stimulus, like the mailman at the door, or it can be an alert asking for help. In the pack, though, dogs do not normally communicate with each other by barking. Rather, when a pack starts barking, the entire group is responding to an outside stimulus or threat.

A dog's barking should not be completely discouraged, of course, and it is very useful in the proper time and place. I have heard more than one police officer say that a dog with a deep, aggressive-sounding bark is the best home security system in the world. Dogs have used their bark to warn humans of other dangers, such as house fires, and some service dogs use barking to warn their handlers of medical conditions, like an imminent epileptic seizure or low blood sugar.

These are examples of proper times and places. However, we do not want our dog to bark constantly for no apparent reason, or to continue barking long after an appropriate moment has passed. Such excessive barking can cause damage to your dog's vocal cords. It can also cause problems with the neighbors, and lead to fines or confiscation of the dog.

EXCESSIVE BARKING: THE CAUSES

Like I said, dogs bark for many reasons, but excessive barking has a variety of causes, including pent-up energy, frustration, separation anxiety, or boredom. Obsessive barking is the manifestation of a dog saying, "My needs are not being met" over and over and over again. You just need to figure out which needs these are, provide the correction, and fulfill those needs.

OVERCOMING EXCESSIVE BARKING

First, look at the situation when the barking occurs. If your dog is barking nonstop when you aren't at home, then it may be a sign of separation anxiety, which is dealt with next in this chapter. The key to reducing or eliminating barking when you aren't home is to make sure that your dog is balanced through

FROM CESAR'S CASE FILES

Kuma

I dealt with a typical case of excessive barking for Jason Zulauf, a performer for Cirque du Soleil's Las Vegas show *KÀ*. His American Eskimo dog, Kuma, would bark at everything, particularly visitors, and would not stop when corrected, only quieting down when she had worn herself out. Jason describes his character in the show as a somewhat buffoonish but lovable clown, an exaggerated version of himself. Unfortunately, he was bringing that character and that energy home with him, leaving Kuma to fill the leadership gap. I began by teaching Jason how to use calm, assertive energy to claim ownership of his space, particularly around the front door. He had also not been exercising Kuma enough, although I will admit that this can be a challenge in a place like Vegas, with its extreme summer climate. Jason and Kuma did show improvement. A few months later, although she was not completely rehabilitated, her barking behavior was minimized, and more under Jason's control. ▪

my fulfillment formula: Exercise, Discipline, then Affection, in that order. Exercise your dog with a vigorous walk before you leave the house, provide a place for the dog to go when you aren't home, and then provide affection well after you've returned and when your dog has reached a calm, submissive state.

If the dog is barking while you are present, there's a lot more you can do to deal with the problem, beginning with staying calm while trying to provide correction. All too often, I will see a person correct a dog by loudly yelling, "NO!" Especially in the case of barking, this will get you nowhere. Why? Because an already excited dog isn't hearing a correction. Rather, he is hearing you joining in the barking by making a loud noise yourself. By trying to fix the problem by adding to the noise, you are just encouraging the behavior.

Start by correcting your dog and stopping the barking with a look, a sound like "Tsch!," or a touch. As long as the barking continues, the corrections continue, but in a calm and assertive manner. You can actually get better results with a very low and quiet "No" that is clearly directed at the dog, because this sounds closer to a warning growl than a loud bark, and it does not exhibit excited energy on your part.

If your dog continues to bark at the same stimulus even after you've tried correcting her, then claim that stimulus as your own. In other words, use your energy, body language, and intent to direct your dog's focus away from it, effectively creating a barrier between her and the cause of the barking. Also, by directing your attention away from the cause of the barking, you are telling your dog that it is of no concern to you.

The cause of the barking also provides an important clue about your dog's state of mind. If she's off at the end of the yard incessantly barking at the neighbors, it means that she is being intellectually fulfilled by whatever is going on over there and she is not being fulfilled at home. She is looking for excitement and a challenge, and finding it elsewhere. Once again, it is time to make sure she is getting enough exercise through the walk and has enough to interest her at home so that she doesn't go looking for it elsewhere. If you find yourself not having any luck stopping the excessive barking yourself, don't hesitate to call in a dog professional.

Like chewing, barking is a natural behavior for dogs, but it can become a problem when it is excessive or comes at inappropriate times. Depending on the underlying cause, you should be able to correct the behavior by providing your dog with fulfillment through the Exercise, Discipline, Affection formula, and your calm, assertive leadership.

 MISBEHAVIOR #9:
Separation Anxiety

In the wild, it is unnatural for members to leave the pack, so it is not normal for dogs when their people leave home. Although many dogs may show mild signs of anxiety when their people walk out the door, it does not escalate further, and they are able to occupy themselves until their pack returns. For some dogs, though, the absence of their humans is too much, and they develop what is known as separation anxiety. In severe cases, a dog may even show signs when a person leaves the room.

Separation anxiety shows itself in symptoms such as excessive salivation, whining, barking, destructiveness, escape attempts, defecating or urinating in the home or crate, or scratching at walls or doors. In some extreme cases, dogs have even jumped through windows.

It is important to treat separation anxiety as soon as you become aware of it, because it can be a very destructive thing, both for your home and property and for your dog. A dog suffering from separation anxiety can destroy furniture, shoes, clothes, papers, computers, and more. The dog can damage walls, doors, and floors, and break windows. He can definitely injure himself

Separation anxiety is more than just "missing you."

in his frantic efforts to escape. Finally, a dog's incessant whining or barking can lead to complaints by neighbors and a visit from animal control. In some areas, dogs that make excessive noise can be taken away and impounded.

SEPARATION ANXIETY: THE CAUSES

Separation anxiety happens when a dog has excess energy but has not been given direction on how to behave when apart from the human pack. Consequently, when the pack leaves, the dog will do everything she can to call the pack back or to follow where it went. Separation anxiety can be made worse if, instead of providing discipline, the humans give the dog affection on the way out the door. With the dog already in an unbalanced state, affection just reinforces the negative energy. In effect, you are telling the dog, "Remain anxious, because it's a good thing." You are not insulting your dog by not saying goodbye. When two dogs interact, they end the meeting by simply walking away from each other. That is the normal way for dogs.

OVERCOMING SEPARATION ANXIETY

The best thing you can do for your dog's separation anxiety is to drain the energy fueling it. When your dog wakes up in the morning, her energy level may be at a 10. Your goal is to drain it to zero with a long walk or exercise before you go anywhere else for the day. When a dog's energy level hits zero, this signals that it is time to rest.

You can prepare a dog for this by training her to "go to your space," letting her settle in her bed or crate, and then walking away. The goal is for you to be able to leave the room without the dog moving from that space. Start small, leaving for a minute or so, and then work your way up. When you can get the dog to stay in the space quietly for 15 minutes, start leaving the house, again working your way up. Start with 5 minutes, then 10, 15, 30.

You may find that your dog does not stay in the space when you are gone for longer times. However, if you have associated that space with your absence, the dog will not leave to try to find you. Rather, she may get up to investigate a noise, get a drink of water, or just to stretch, returning to that space afterward.

When it comes to actually leaving the home, say goodbye to your dog long before you go. When she is calm and submissive, and after her exercise, it's all right to give a little affection and tell her you'll miss her while you're gone. Of course, this is more for your benefit than hers. Remember, dogs don't naturally say goodbye to each other. After you have done what you've had to

FROM CESAR'S CASE FILES

Fella

I was once called in to deal with a dog's separation anxiety because it was literally endangering the entire family's living situation. After neighbors had complained multiple times about the dog's incessant whining, Cindy Steiner and her daughter Sydney were one complaint away from being evicted. Their dog, a year-and-a-half-old terrier mix named Fella, exhibited extreme separation anxiety whenever he was left alone. He was also aggressive toward other dogs, and exhibited protective behavior whenever Cindy was holding him, growling and nipping at anyone who approached her. Luckily, using the techniques I'm about to describe, Cindy and Sydney were able to teach Fella to go into a resting state before his human pack left the apartment, and I showed them how to use a crate to create a safe space for him to go into. It took them about three and a half weeks to turn Fella around, but they are still living in the same apartment, and the neighbors cannot believe it's the same dog. ▪

so that you feel better, go about the rest of your routine, practicing the "No Touch, No Talk, No Eye Contact" approach. If you don't make a big deal about getting ready to go, your dog won't either.

In nature, dogs are almost never away from their pack, so separation from their humans can be very stressful. It is our job to reduce the energy that fuels separation anxiety, and to create a safe place for our dog to be in our absence. When using the previous tips, remember to project calm, assertive energy. This will build your dog's confidence and help to further minimize her anxiety. Above all, make clear to your dog your expectations of where she should be and what she should do while you are gone by creating a safe place associated with restful energy.

Misbehavior #10: Unwanted Chewing

Chewing is practically synonymous with normal dog behavior and, done in the proper way and with appropriate objects, is actually a good thing to encourage. It can help strengthen and clean your dog's teeth, give an intellectual challenge, and in the case of puppies, alleviate teething pain and ease the transition from infant to adult teeth.

However, when dogs unleash their teeth on inappropriate objects, then such behavior becomes one of the biggest head-aches for dog lovers. You may have experienced the feeling—coming home to find pieces of your favorite pair of shoes scattered all over the living room; that irreplaceable needlepoint pillow wedding present from Aunt Maggie shredded; the charger for your laptop turned into a cordless lump of plastic.

In such situations, though, disciplining the dog on the spot does no good. Chances are, the dog has already forgotten about what he chewed up, and he won't relate your sudden scolding to the feathers scattered all over the house.

In fact, discipline here may make matters worse. Your yelling at him for no apparent reason may just make him nervous, and chewing may be his way of calming down. If you mis-time the discipline, you may be saying goodbye to another favorite shoe.

Inappropriate chewing can also be very dangerous for a dog. A dog may break something into small pieces and swallow them, where they can cause problems in the esophagus, stomach, or intestines. She may get hold of a power cord that's plugged in, possibly burning or electrocuting herself or starting a fire. Beyond physical danger to the dog, there are also the financial costs of replacing expensive items and emotional costs of losing items that are not replaceable at all.

So the challenge here is to make sure that an absolutely natural and healthy activity for a dog remains targeted at the right objects without you having to stick everything you own in high places or behind locked doors whenever you leave the house.

Unwanted Chewing: The Causes

Most frequently, adult dogs use chewing to calm themselves and give their minds something interesting to do. It may be a hold-over from their teething behavior as puppies, during which the action of chewing would have helped soothe the pain in their gums from new teeth coming in. The association with "ending an unpleasant feeling" from puppyhood may be enough to bring an adult dog back to a calm and submissive state. Calm and sub-missive is very good; it's what you want. You just shouldn't have to get it at the expense of your stuff being destroyed.

Overcoming Unwanted Chewing

It is easier to correct this behavior if you catch your dog with the inappropriate object in her mouth, as you can then associate the correction directly with the behavior. This is not to encourage entrapping your dog by leaving a sock out, however. It just explains what to do if you do catch your dog chewing something he shouldn't be.

I've already discussed the importance of remaining calm. Give the dog a correction with a light, gentle touch of your fingers on the neck or hindquarters. This is meant to turn your dog's attention away from the object. Do not try to take away the object unless your dog drops it upon correction. If she doesn't drop it, then redirect her attention with an appropriate object, like a chew toy or a treat, which should get her to drop the object and take the approved item instead.

Once your dog has dropped the object, claim it as yours. Use your energy and body language to establish a connection between you and the object, and make it clear to the dog that the object is yours. It helps if you imagine an invisible boundary around you and the object. You can also pick it up and hold it close to your body while showing calm, assertive energy, physically saying quite clearly, "Mine." If you ever observe two dogs deciding which one gets a lone toy, you'll see that the dog that wins usually does so using nothing more than body language and energy, without resorting to growling or aggression. That dog will simply position herself over the object and then give the other dog a warning look. This is the dog's way of saying, "Mine."

If your dog or puppy is a chewer, then by all means provide her with safe, appropriate chew toys. Consult your veterinarian regarding edible objects, such as bones, rawhide, or other chews. Make sure other rubber or plastic toys are big enough that your dog cannot swallow them, and that they are not large enough that your dog can get her face or jaw stuck inside, especially if they have a hole in them. Be especially careful about toys designed to hide treats inside. Though they are typically fine, be absolutely certain that the toy has holes in both ends—one for your dog to try to get the treat out of, and another to let air flow in so that there's no chance of creating a vacuum and trapping your dog's tongue inside. The airhole should be at least the diameter of your pinkie.

Adult humans have 32 teeth, but adult dogs have ten more than that. Additionally, a dog's front teeth are pointier and sharper than ours, and their jaws, back where the grinding molars are, are much more powerful than a human's. A human being may crack a molar by biting an ice cube. Dogs can easily snap a bone in half with their molars. So, biologically, it's obvious that dogs are quite capable of chewing; psychologically, dogs find the action calming and interesting. You should not discourage your dog from appropriate chewing, but you should never let a dog continue the habit of chewing inappropriate objects.

▶A Solid Foundation

All dogs will misbehave from time to time. But with the techniques in this chapter, you'll be well on your way to addressing problems when they come up. Coupled with the laws, principles, and techniques from earlier chapters, you should have a solid foundation and methods for creating balance in your pack—no matter what comes up.

All of these tools come into play in every aspect of your relationship with your dog. But did you know that you can use them in your life before you even have a dog? In the next chapter, I'm going to show how to apply all these practices as you search for the perfect dog to fit your lifestyle and energy.

CHAPTER SIX

Choosing the Right Dog for You

I got a call one Saturday afternoon from my good friend, the movie producer Barry Josephson. I have known Barry for about ten years. We met in the parking lot of a restaurant back in 2000, way before I had a TV show and before anyone knew who Cesar Millan was. He became one of my very first "celebrity" clients.

I had a pack of about 12 dogs in the back of my old van. I hadn't noticed Barry, but he noticed me as I gave each dog a command to jump out of my parked van. Each dog waited patiently until I gave the command. Barry was impressed. I have trained all of Barry's dogs since.

Two of Barry's dogs had recently passed away, and Barry was still hurting from the loss. Barry's third dog, a purebred pit bull by the name of Gusto, was also sad. Barry went on to explain that his wife, Brooke, felt that Gusto was in such pain that she needed to get another dog. Barry pleaded with her to wait until I returned from an overseas trip so I could help the family find the right match. However, Brooke couldn't take it anymore and went to a rescue organization to adopt a puppy. Unfortunately for Brooke, the rescuers gave her a high-energy dog that wasn't compatible with Gusto. When Brooke brought the puppy home, he began nipping at their three-year-old daughter, Shira. Of course, Gusto wouldn't stand for that and stepped in to protect Shira from the puppy. From that day on, Gusto ignored the puppy. Although the Josephsons realized that the puppy was not a good match for their family, they decided to foster it (keeping it safely away from Shira, of course) until they could find him the right home.

This kind of story is repeated thousands of times because humans don't understand the full process of how to select a dog that's right for them. It's not as simple as going to a shelter and picking out a dog—there are lots of variables to consider. For example, compatible energy attracts. Incompatible energy can be a disaster. Combine incompatibility with improperly introducing a new dog to your pack, and you have the formula for a sad but all-too-common situation of a rescued dog being returned to the shelter. When you adopt a dog, you are making a promise to care for him for his life. You owe it to that dog to do your homework and choose very carefully.

As I see it, choosing a dog has three key phases: self-assessment, dog assessment, and, ultimately, homeward bound.

PHASE 1: Self-Assessment

This phase begins with an honest look at yourself and your life. You must consider many different parts of your life and how a dog can best fit into it.

SELF-ASSESSMENT #1:
It's a Family Affair

When you decide to get a new dog, that decision must involve every member of your human pack, because each of you will have to be the Pack Leader. Everyone should be in agreement about getting a new dog. If Dad has promised a dog for the kids but Mom objects to that decision, this can cause problems down the line, particularly if the kids grow bored with their responsibilities and Mom winds up being the one feeding and walking the dog she didn't want in the first place. Have frank conversations with each other about a dog and what family members can realistically be expected to contribute.

Here are the kinds of questions you should be thinking about:

- If you have children, are they old enough for the responsibility of sharing in leadership and caretaker roles? If they are not old enough for that, are they old enough to understand that a dog is not a toy and to respect the dog's space?
- Do the children understand that the dog is part of the entire family and doesn't "belong" to one child more than to any other?
- Will there always be someone at home with the dog, or does the entire family take off early in the morning and return in the evening?
- Is the family used to taking regular vacations? If so, will you alter your methods of travel and accommodations so you can take your dog with you? What will you do if the dog stays home? Do you have

responsible friends, family, or a trusted kennel that can care for your dog while you're away?

- Does anyone in the family have allergies that would make adopting certain kinds of dogs impossible? (If so, you should investigate hypoallergenic breeds, such as the Portuguese water dog.)

SELF-ASSESSMENT #2:
Look at Your Living Space

Before you begin your search, you've got to understand the "rules, boundaries, and limitations" of your living space. Make sure that you will be allowed to have dogs where you live. Check your lease if you rent or read the bylaws of your homeowners association for any pet restrictions. Lastly, make sure that you know the local laws regarding dogs in your community.

Next, take a quick look around you. What is your living situation? Tiny apartment or large house and yard? A suburban or rural neighborhood with great walking trails and lots of nature, or a big city with sparse patches of grass and lots of traffic? When thinking about your new dog, try to imagine what kind of dog will fit in well with your living space. A high-energy dog in cramped quarters will most likely be a bad match.

Then consider the layout of your home. Do you have rooms in the house that will be off-limits to a dog? If so, what is your plan for restricting access? Will your dog be allowed on the furniture or not? Where will the dog spend most of her time? Coming up with your "house rules" before you start searching will help you get a better sense of what kind of companion you're looking for.

SELF-ASSESSMENT #3:
Consider Your Energy

You also need to consider your family's lifestyle and energy level. Are you a pack of couch potatoes who prefer time in front of the TV, computer, or video game right after dinner and don't move until bedtime? Or are you an active family, up at dawn every weekend and off for a hike, or to the beach or other adventure? You should never adopt a dog with a higher energy level than your own pack—unless you are willing to change your lifestyle to accommodate that dog's energy. A high-energy Dalmatian or Jack Russell terrier would be a bad choice for a low-energy family but would thrive with early-rising hikers.

Take an honest look at the emotional state of your family. This is probably the most important factor of all, because the energy in your household will greatly affect your dog's behavior. On many of my cases, I could take one look at the dog and instantly know that there was trouble in the primary relationship in the household.

You have to be honest and determine whether there are any unresolved issues in the family dynamic, whether between spouses, between siblings, or between parents and children. Dogs will easily pick up on unbalanced energy and, sensing trouble in the pack, will try to take a leadership role. This frequently plays out as the dog trying to "protect" the stronger human pack member from the weaker one by becoming possessive and, sometimes, aggressive.

Rosie, the Stressed-Out Staffie

One month before we began filming the show *Cesar Millan's Leader of the Pack*, Executive Producer Gregory Vanger and my training assistant, Cheri Lucas, flew to London to begin dog selection for the show. Their first stop was Animal Helpline in Peterborough, England. As at many shelters, the volunteer staff there doesn't possess the knowledge to resolve many of the behavioral issues they have to contend with.

During a tour of the facility, Cheri met Rosie, a gorgeous Staffordshire terrier. Relinquished to a high-kill shelter by her first family, Rosie was scheduled to be put down within a few days, but Animal Helpline pulled her from the pound and took her in.

However, the stress on Rosie was beginning to take its toll. Rosie had developed a noncontagious form of mange from the stress. She was placed again into a loving home, but her new human developed a severe allergy to her and ended up in the hospital for anaphylactic shock. Reluctantly, Rosie was returned to Animal Helpline . . . again.

So, thanks to Cheri, Rosie became part of the *Leader of the Pack* crew! A few weeks later, Rosie was on a plane to our Dog Psychology Center in Spain, with no idea of the adventure that awaited her. Once she arrived, we started the serious effort of tackling Rosie's mange. Rosie's behavioral issues were mild, but she had become very skilled at manipulating humans. Before, she had no rules and no boundaries, and if she didn't want to walk, well, she was going nowhere.

My staff and I were able to rehabilitate Rosie very quickly. It didn't take any time at all for us to turn her around—all it took was a strong leader. But now, we needed to match Rosie with a new family. The question was: Who fit that profile?

Several candidates were competing to adopt Rosie, including a cancer survivor named Debbie and a family with two children. Debbie was on a journey to turn her life around—not only had she battled cancer but she had also faced down obesity and severe depression. Debbie decided to appear on *Leader of the Pack* to find a dog to be part of her brand-new life. The production team favored the family with two adorable children, as they wanted Rosie to have the loving, stable family she deserved.

However, I decided that Rosie would be a better fit for Debbie. I believed that Debbie and Rosie were of a singular mind—both needed rehabilitation, and they would be just enough of a challenge for each other that their love and appreciation would grow through the process of healing. I am happy to report that as I write this, Rosie and Debbie are doing very well together. Debbie is committed to the process of helping Rosie become the perfect canine companion, and Rosie seems to be giving new purpose to Debbie. ▪

SELF-ASSESSMENT #4:
What's in Your Wallet?

It is supposed to be impolite to talk about money, but you do have to seriously consider whether the family can afford a dog. Taking proper care of a pet costs money. In addition to the initial costs of adoption, microchipping, licensing, accessories, and spaying or neutering, you will have monthly expenses for food and annual expenses for veterinary care. These can vary by type and size of dog, and by your location, but the American Society for the Prevention of Cruelty to Animals (ASPCA) estimates the average monthly expense for dog necessities at about $70.

This figure doesn't include veterinary expenses or pet insurance. If you don't have pet insurance, then you should at least have a savings account set aside with a few thousand dollars in disposable income in case of a sudden emergency. Like people, pets do get hurt and they do get sick. Having that safety net can take some worry out of the equation while your dog is recovering.

PHASE 2: Dog Assessment

Once you have made an honest assessment of your family lifestyle, energy level, and dynamics, then it is time to start considering what kind of dog you should bring into your pack.

DOG ASSESSMENT #1:
Age Is More Than Just a Number

Puppies are cute and adorable and hard to find at shelters because they're first to be adopted, but the reality is that puppies also require a much bigger investment of time, energy, and money to bring into a household. Many behavioral issues that later require professional help have their roots in how a puppy is raised. Unless you or a family member is able to be around all the time for a couple of months to over a year, and is able to spend that time in consistent training, then a puppy is not the ideal choice.

Dogs reach adulthood between a year and 18 months of age, and if they've been properly raised to that point, they are less likely to come with issues. At the very least, you should be able to spot potential issues in a meet and greet at the shelter or rescue group and decide whether you're willing to deal with fixing them. Adult dogs are also much more likely to be housebroken, and depending upon temperament and breed, their energy levels are generally lower than those of puppies. If you don't have as much time to dedicate to a dog, then an adult under seven years of age is a good choice.

Don't count out senior dogs, though. Generally the last ones to be adopted from a shelter, they will still be with you for years, and are frequently more balanced and lower energy than their younger counterparts. If you have limited space and not as much time to dedicate to training and walking a dog, then a mellow old senior may be the perfect match for your household. The trade-off is that you're likely to face higher veterinary expenses—but an older dog is ideal for someone with no children in the house, like a single person or married couple whose kids have all moved out.

Don't forget to take your own age and energy level into account when considering a dog to adopt. A high-energy puppy might be too much for a senior citizen to handle, whereas an older dog might not be able to keep up with an energetic 20-something. Again, you should only adopt a dog with the same or lower energy level than your human pack. Considering all the options when it comes to age will maximize your chances of finding the right dog.

DOG ASSESSMENT #2: **Know Your Breeds**

I've explained that dogs should be seen as animal, species, breed, and then name, in that order, but breed can move higher in importance when adopting and making lifestyle matching decisions. The purer the breed, the more likely a dog will strongly exhibit traits particular to that breed, and therefore have specific needs.

In Chapter 3, I discussed the seven groups of dogs: sporting, hound, working, herding, terrier, toy, and nonsporting (see page 62). To fulfill dogs in all of these groups, it may be necessary to give them a job appropriate to their breed instincts. Sporting dogs may require a lot of time playing fetch, for example, whereas working dogs may be happiest wearing a backpack on the walk. Terriers frequently need stimulating mental challenges and love to work for rewards, so they may need toys that allow them to "find the treat." Hounds can be tireless runners, so they make a great match if you love to jog, skate, or ride a bicycle.

When considering a new dog, it helps to do your homework, particularly if you find yourself drawn to a particular breed. You'll find many published sources on dog breeds, both in book form and online, and American Kennel Club (AKC) breed standards regarding temperament are an excellent guide on what to expect.

Unfortunately, we live in a world with breed-specific laws; many apartment buildings and homeowners associations will not allow particular breeds, so you need to do your research in this area, too. Although aggression is a trait of an animal with unbalanced energy, it is sadly also often attributed to a handful of breeds, regardless of a particular dog's behavior or temperament. Sometimes it doesn't even matter whether dogs are purebred members of a particular breed; if they look like an aggressive breed, they are considered aggressive, period. Lennox was a mixed-breed dog in the United Kingdom that vaguely resembled a pit bull and had no reports of aggressive behavior. His breed status alone was enough for the Belfast City Council to seize and, ultimately, destroy him in 2012, despite international protests. Again, do your homework first to be informed about any dogs that may run afoul of these perceptions and laws.

Finally, consider possible medical issues that certain breeds are prone to—for example, hip dysplasia in German shepherds, or thyroid problems in Pomeranians. Again, the purer the breed, the more likely they are to have problems typical of that breed. Research the possible expenses of treatment in a worst-case scenario, and then add that into the likely financial costs of adopting a dog.

If you take the time to learn about breeds—their needs, issues, and energy levels—then you'll have a much better idea of what you're looking for on your search, and adopt responsibly.

DOG ASSESSMENT #3:
Select the Right Energy

I've mentioned several times in this and other chapters that you should adopt a dog with the right energy for your household, but how do you determine what a dog's natural energy level is? Visiting a shelter, where the dogs are kept in cages, can be misleading, because a dog in such a situation can build up frustrated, edgy energy that is not reflective of his normal state.

Take advantage of the volunteers and staff at the shelter, and ask questions about dogs you're interested in. Chances are, they have spent a good amount of time with all of the dogs and have a better idea of their general temperament and behavior. Shelter workers don't get a commission for adopting out dogs and they know that bad matches will probably wind up right back in the shelter, so it's to their benefit to be honest and informative.

Questions to ask include the following: How does the dog get along with staff members and other dogs? How does the dog behave at mealtime and on the walk? How does the dog react to visitors coming up to the cage? Does she seem to have any issues with particular people, such as children or men?

When you think you've found a possibility, then your entire family should visit the shelter for the aforementioned "meet and greet." Most shelters are happy to have you do this, and have a designated area where everyone can gather with the dog off leash. Observing the dog outside of the kennel and with some degree of freedom can also tell you a lot. Is the dog easily distracted by everything? Does he investigate each new person or seem to fixate on only one? Does he immediately begin to mark all around the meeting area? Is he outgoing or timid? Is he constantly in motion, or does he settle down quickly and demonstrate calm, submissive energy?

Finally, if the shelter or rescue allows it, the best way to gauge whether a dog's energy and personality will be a good fit is to take her on a walk; think of this as a "test drive." This will give you an idea of whether the dog has issues with pulling or trying to lead you. If you can take a sufficiently long walk to drain the dog's energy, you will also get an idea of her real temperament outside of the kennel.

Most important, you should remain as objective as possible during this process. You will have plenty of time to fall in love with the dog later, but that will be a lot easier if you find the right dog in the first place. It can be easy to fall for the first dog that catches your eye and then adopt out of guilt because you don't want to leave her in the shelter, but this can lead to bad choices. You really don't want to bring home that high-energy Saint Bernard puppy if you live in a studio apartment and work 12-hour days.

A dog is not a toy or a piece of furniture. A dog is a lifetime commitment. It is far better to turn down the options that will not be good fits and find the dog with the right temperament and energy level for you than to adopt the wrong dog and later have to make the hard decision to give her up or bring her back. With the right questions and observations—and patience—you can maximize your chances of finding that perfect match.

Sofia, the Fearful Italian Dog

S ofia was one of the most heart-wrenching cases we ever dealt with on *Leader of the Pack.* Cheri Lucas flew into Rome with a mere 24 hours to find the perfect canine candidate for the show. An Italian producer whom we had hired to shoot footage of the Italian dogs for the show met her there, and they drove an hour outside of Rome to a shelter in the Italian countryside that housed over 400 dogs. Of these 400 dogs, nearly half were senior dogs. Another quarter of the dogs were pit bulls or pit mixes—highly undesirable dogs in Italy. The rest had severe issues: either dog or human aggression, fear, or antisocial behavior. And then there was Sofia . . .

Sofia was not on the "short list"—a list of dogs compiled for the show prior to visiting Italy. We already had a "fear case," so we were on a quest to find a different kind of issue that would add more interest to the show.

As Cheri tells the story, "When I walked by Sofia's run, she was surrounded by other runs full of dogs that were barking incessantly, throwing themselves at the fence, or spinning in their runs. She was terrified. Sofia had the biggest, most soulful eyes I had ever seen. I was smitten. One look at Sofia and all you wanted to do was help her.

"One of the shelter staff allowed me to enter Sofia's run. I attempted to get a leash on Sofia, but she was in a complete panic by my presence. I knew what to do—no eye contact, no attempt to touch her, no baby talking, but it didn't matter. Sofia's level of terror was so intense, I thought at one point that she would collapse."

Sofia's backstory was very sad. Her owner had been incarcerated on unknown charges. Authorities then found over a dozen dogs in his backyard. All of them were adults, and each seemed to be part of the same litter. All of these dogs had been equally neglected—each of them was terrified. The rest of Sofia's siblings remained at the shelter.

Cheri finally got a leash on Sofia and began the process of removing her from the run. "She was completely shut down, but eventually I got her out. At this point, she collapsed. The only way I could return her to her run was to carry her. Sixty-five pounds of dead weight is a lot to carry, but eventually I got her back in her run."

Fortunately, the show agreed to take on Sofia. Once Sofia arrived in Spain, she began to change almost overnight. The serene, peaceful atmosphere at Centro Canino in Madrid began to work its magic on Sofia. Within a few days, we filmed my first attempts at rehabilitating Sofia.

Continued on next page . . .

Sofia, continued . . .

I found that bringing the balanced pack of over a dozen dogs into the mix with Sofia was part of the answer to her recovery. All that Sofia had ever known was other dogs, so it was only logical to use them to help Sofia move forward.

Out of the three couples that applied for Sofia, I was particularly interested in one young couple, Danilo and Sara, from Bologna, Italy. Danilo was a "cat person" and had never really had a dog before. I was fascinated by the fact that this man was so in love with cats, his own very spoiled cat, in particular. Danilo was concerned that adopting a dog would upset the cat. I found this kind of amusing, but also recognized the seriousness of bringing a dog into a home with a rather spoiled feline.

In this particular case, the other two candidates were clearly not cut out for a case that was going to require lots of commitment. They had very active and busy lives, and they were looking for a dog to provide companionship. Sofia's fear was going to improve only if her adoptive family was willing to put time and effort into her rehabilitation.

Needless to say, Sara and Danilo are doing great with Sofia. However, after visiting a veterinarian upon arrival to her new home, it was discovered that Sofia has a rare condition called pulmonary hypertension. The condition is impossible to detect without an extensive veterinary exam, but our production team is standing behind Sofia's care and offering assistance to the young couple who adopted her. ▪

PHASE 3: Homeward Bound!

So you've gone through all the pre-adoption steps, visited the shelters, and found the perfect match. Congratulations on the new member of your pack! Here are three other very important things you need to do next.

HOMEWARD BOUND #1: Spay or Neuter Your Dog

Now we're going to talk about the bird dogs and the beagles, so you might want to send the young ones out of the room . . .

In many places, all dogs adopted from city or county shelters must be spayed or neutered before they will be released, and this is usually included in the adoption fees. There are exceptions for registered and licensed breeders, but the license fees for intact dogs are also generally a lot higher. In the city of Los Angeles, for example, the annual license fee for a spayed or neutered dog is only $20, but the fee for a dog that is not fixed is $100, plus a $235 permit fee, and microchipping is mandatory.

Unless you are a professional and responsible breeder, there is no good argument for not having your dog fixed. Unlike humans, who may mate at any time, male dogs only feel the urge strongly when there are female dogs in heat nearby, and females go into heat only twice a year—typically between January and March, and again between August and October. Otherwise, your dogs really won't know or care what they're missing. Despite the existence of products like Neuticles, which are meant to replace a male dog's missing parts, Rover really won't sit around feeling sorry for what's gone, and such cosmetic "un-fixes" are really more for the human's benefit than the dog's.

Having your dog fixed can also be healthier for them down the line, particularly for female dogs. Early sterilization can prevent mammary tumors and urinary tract infections. For both male and female dogs, eliminating hormone signals can lead to a more even and predictable temperament. It will also prevent them from trying to escape during mating season and then presenting you with an unwanted and unexpected litter of puppies.

Financially, sterilization is a small investment with a bigger payoff down the line, and many shelters and clinics offer low-cost or free sterilization programs. Again, many shelters include the procedure as part of the adoption fees.

The most important reason to spay or neuter, though, is pet overpopulation. Four to five million unwanted dogs and cats are destroyed every year due to overpopulation in the United States. Worldwide, there are six hundred million stray dogs. Sterilization is the single most effective way to deal with this problem. I saw the results firsthand while visiting Germany during production of *Leader of the Pack*. In that country, people with dogs—except for breeders—are required to have their pets sterilized; because of this, Germany does not have the stray dog problem that the United States has. In fact, the country has reduced the problem so much that it is now taking in shelter dogs from other countries.

When it comes to being a responsible dog owner, you must provide many things—food, shelter, guidance, training, and leadership. But the kindest thing you can do, for your dog and for yourself, is to guarantee that you will not create a generation of unwanted pups. The decision on whether to spay or neuter should be a no-brainer. It's a simple, safe, and inexpensive procedure that will prevent many problems throughout your dog's lifetime.

☑ HOMEWARD BOUND #2:
Microchipping Is a Must

Once upon a time, the only available ID systems for dogs were tags on their collars or tattooing, which was never as popular or common. Both methods have drawbacks. Runaway dogs can easily lose their collars or tags, or thieves can remove these IDs. Likewise, tattoos can be removed or altered.

In the 1990s, this changed with the advent of the RFID (radio frequency identification) chip, a tiny, implantable device that can last up to 25 years. The chip is encoded with a unique number that will identify your dog and help reunite her with you in case she is lost. When your dog is microchipped and registered, it is very easy to establish ownership if someone finds or steals her and tries to claim the dog for themselves.

Like spaying and neutering, microchipping will ultimately help reduce the stray dog problem. Although some people are disturbed by the idea of implantable identification, the benefits really do outweigh the drawbacks. After all, we don't complain that cars have to have license plates, and your dog is a lot more valuable to you than your car, right?

The chips themselves are harmless, passive devices. Unlike cell phones or other electronics, RFID chips do not transmit anything on their own. They never emit any kind of harmful radiation. They become active only in the presence of a scanner, which sends out a signal to which the chip responds with the number encoded in it. This process takes only a few seconds.

As the chips become more common and technology in general improves, we are beginning to see some interesting alternate uses for this form of ID. For example, one company now manufactures a dog door that uses its own scanner to read the RFID chip. If it recognizes your dog, then the door unlocks; otherwise, it does not. Now, instead of an inviting flap providing entry for the neighbors' dogs, roving raccoons, or opportunistic burglars, you can in effect give your dog his own personal key.

There is another, very humane reason to seriously consider microchipping—a dog with such an ID cannot be abandoned. In the past, people who wanted to dump a dog would only have to remove his collar and tags, drive him to a remote area, and let him out of the car. A dog with a microchip, though, will lead authorities right back to the registered owner. RFID also provides a way to track down people responsible for training dogs for fighting or to be human-aggressive. Like a gun with a serial number, an owner of a dog recovered from a fighting ring or captured in connection with a crime can be tracked down and held responsible.

The process of microchipping is quick, as painless as a vaccination, and cheap; like spaying and neutering, it is becoming more commonly included in the cost of adoption. Look at it this way: If you have your dog microchipped, you will never regret doing it, but if you don't and your dog gets lost, you will forever regret that you didn't.

HOMEWARD BOUND #3:
Meeting Your Human Pack

You've located the perfect dog with the right energy for your family and lifestyle. You've researched the breed, decided you can handle any special needs, and have everyone in the household ready to take on the role of Pack Leader. You go through the adoption process, including microchipping and spaying or neutering, and today is the big day—time to bring home your new dog.

This is the point in the process when many people make the biggest mistake, frequently out of excitement over having a new family member. They drive home, bring the dog out of the car and to the front door, throw the door open, take off the leash, and let the dog loose to explore her new home . . . and the poor dog has no idea what's going on or where she is. It may look like she's excitedly investigating as she runs from room to room, sniffing everywhere, but she isn't. You've just thrown her into a completely alien environment with no direction, and these early associations are going to stick. The place is unfamiliar, it smells different, and there doesn't seem to be any way out. If you have previously had pets in the house, it will smell like them, and your new dog will be uncertain about invading someone else's territory.

So let's back up from the front door and back to the car, and back to the shelter. Before you even bring the dog to the car, take her on an energetic walk. This will help use up the pent-up energy from being in the shelter. Once you are in the car, stop a few blocks from home and take your dog on another walk, this time to your doorstep. This allows her to get used to the smells and sights of the new neighborhood and to begin to feel confident about being there. She will also get to know you and your energy, and you will begin to establish trust.

Finally, when you arrive home, it's not time to let your new dog go bounding inside yet. Lead her to whichever door you enter through, and then make her sit, waiting until she shows calm, submissive energy. When you open the door, you and the family must enter first. Only then, invite your new dog in, but keep her on the lead for now—and make sure that everyone practices "No Touch, No Talk, No Eye Contact" (see Chapter 2, page 45).

The idea is that you slowly introduce your new dog to her new place, one room at a time, and you should begin with the room where she will find her food and water, making her wait until you have gone through the door and invited her in. Have her sit while you get her food and water ready. After she has eaten, she should be even more relaxed. Now you can give her the tour of the rest of the house, avoiding rooms you do not want her to enter.

As with that first room, make her wait at the threshold to every room until you invite her in. Keeping her on the lead, let her sniff and explore each new place before leading her to the next. What you are doing with this process is telling the dog,

"This is my territory. I own it, but I am allowing you in." It will help build your dog's respect for what is yours from the beginning.

Once you have completed the tour, it will be time for your new dog to meet each of the human members of the pack, one at a time. Let her smell them first, and don't allow anyone to show affection until the new dog comes to them. Pack Leaders do not go to their followers; their followers come to them.

HOMEWARD BOUND #4:
Introductions to Your Canine Pack

If you already have a dog at home, you need to manage the introduction of the new dog to your current pet. Don't just throw the two of them together. Although the kids may be excited to have a new puppy in the house, your existing dog may not be so thrilled. In fact, such an introduction can make your older dog defensive and your newer dog insecure, leading to problems. Look at it from your older dog's point of view: She's just hanging out in her place, minding her own business, when suddenly this strange dog comes running in and the humans seem very excited, so there must be something terrible happening. That's the formula for failure right there.

Introducing a new dog to an existing pack will take the assistance of a friend or family member, but the results are worth it. Simply put, each of you should arrange to meet in neutral territory while walking one of the dogs—you with your current dog, and the other person with the new one. You should encounter each other casually and begin walking together with the dogs on the outside. They may or may not become curious about each other right away, but it's important to keep moving forward for a while, and walk until both dogs have had their energy levels lowered.

Janna, the Belgian Malinois

We traveled to the Netherlands on our search for dogs for the new show. While visiting a shelter outside of Amsterdam, we came across a gorgeous, four-year-old female Belgian Malinois, a herding breed that resembles German shepherds. Janna had been picked up as a stray. She had been microchipped, so the shelter called the owners, but they refused to come pick her up, stating that they no longer wanted her. She was subsequently placed in a home with an elderly man who passed away three years later. Once again, Janna found herself back at the shelter Dierenopvangcentrum Enschede. (Yes, the spelling is correct! Dierenopvangcentrum is Dutch for "animal shelter.") Only this time, Janna had changed.

Janna had become highly stressed at the shelter now. She developed an obsessive behavior of biting her entire hindquarters, hip, and tail, becoming very vocal when starting this behavior. She would continue for several minutes and would not stop until exhausted. This self-mutilating behavior left her covered in her own saliva. We knew we could help Janna overcome her obsession and match her with a good home, so she was selected to be on *Cesar Millan's Leader of the Pack.*

When Janna arrived in Spain, her behavior began to escalate. While in Cheri Lucas's home for an overnight stay, Janna opened cabinet doors and "nested" inside. She dug holes in the backyard and curled up inside of them. This behavior made us concerned that Janna might be pregnant, because most shelters in the Netherlands don't practice regular spaying or neutering.

A trip to the vet determined that Janna wasn't pregnant but suffering from a very intense case of false pregnancy, due to having gone through several heat cycles over the previous four years without having had a litter. The vet determined that the nesting behavior was Janna's determination to find a place to have her imaginary puppies. It was an odd syndrome but, more than that, an almost intolerable condition to have to live with. We started Janna on holistic medications and got her involved in agility exercises to work off her excess energy. Belgians belong to a very high-energy breed that absolutely must be challenged on a daily basis.

Out of the three candidate families that applied for Janna, I was very drawn to one family in particular. This couple from Belgium had one adorable, precocious son. Sven, the father, was disabled due to an industrial accident and was unable to work. He walked with a cane and had chronic pain that left him severely depressed. The young child's unrelenting support of his father touched me. I could see that this family genuinely supported one another.

Although Janna's case was very challenging due to the length of time she would need for rehabilitation, I felt that this family was the right choice for her. I was convinced that Sven would rally to help Janna fully recover, just as he was trying to recover himself from chronic pain. They would be a team. Many tears were shed during the selection process. Even the candidates who were eliminated were touched by this family's struggles and were thrilled that Sven and his family had been selected to adopt Janna. ▪

At this point, you can bring both dogs back to their home, humans entering first and then both dogs invited in. The rest of the introduction process is the same, except that you can now allow your older dog off leash, unless she tries to instigate play with the new dog, in which case both should remain leashed. Although trying to play would be an excellent sign that they're going to get along, save the play as a reward for after the new dog has done the work of following your leadership and learning the new space.

By following these procedures when bringing a new dog into your pack, you will start off on the right paw together by demonstrating pack leadership and setting Rules, Boundaries, and Limitations from the beginning. You will have plenty of time for affection and fun and games later—a lifetime's worth, in fact. But everything you do on that first day will affect everything that happens from there on out. It is worth every ounce of effort to do it right.

CHAPTER SEVEN

Life Changes, Your Dog, and You

Change is an inevitable part of anyone's life. A new home, a new baby, a new partner—these are just a few of the events people experience. During times of change and uncertainty, it's important to keep looking ahead as you move forward. Remember to keep your dog in your plans—transitions affect dogs too. But it has been my experience that dogs tend to handle whatever life throws at them a lot better than humans do.

Dogs are one of the most adaptable creatures God ever created, but humans, however, are another story. We hold on to things like emotions and memories. These "things" make us stuck so that we either live in the past or we're fearful or anxious about the future, and the present . . . is ignored.

People often wonder how I get such quick results with the dogs I rehabilitate. The simple answer is what we talked about in Chapter 3: Dogs live in the moment. They lack anxiety or fear of the future. That's the essence of their surrender state. If we humans can learn to appreciate and focus on what's happening in the here and now, even when we're not sure what the future will bring, we'll experience a richness of living that other members of the animal kingdom enjoy.

You may be wondering why I am talking about humans in a chapter dedicated to helping your dog through life's transitions and changes. It's because humans are one of the main reasons why dogs have difficulty adjusting to change. When big changes occur in our lives, we project our emotions, our sorrows, or our excitement onto our dog. The dog, in essence, becomes our mirror. That's why when I am working with a new client for the first time, I say that the human tells me the "story" with all the emotions, drama, and judgments while the dog tells me the truth about what's really going on. When I approach a dog with a problem for the very first time, I usually see the following pattern:

Humans =
story + emotions + energy + judgment + past/future

Dog =
truth + mirror of human energy + nonjudgment + present

Divorce, death, birth, and new relationships are just some of life's transitions. They affect humans, and in turn, the humans affect the dogs. Dogs do not know what your situation is; they just know that your energy has changed.

Although hundreds, if not thousands, of self-help books exist to help people through these transitions, few books have been written to help dog owners transition their dogs through these life-changing events. With a little advance planning and consideration, you can ease your dog, and yourself, through any transition.

Here are some commonsense tips to help you maintain a healthy, balanced state of mind while the world changes around you.

TRANSITION:
Leaving the House

Leaving the house might not seem like a big transition to you. It's probably something you do every day. But for dogs, who are very social animals, being left alone can be unsettling. It is unusual for dogs to leave the pack in nature. Being left alone in the house can even cause separation anxiety in some dogs (see Chapter 5, page 130). What feels like a small transition to humans can feel like a big transition to dogs.

To maintain balance, you've got to help your dog understand that this part of your daily routine is a normal thing and is nothing to worry about:

1 Rehearse your hellos and goodbyes. Practice going out and coming into the house many times before you actually leave the dog alone for extended periods of time. When leaving your home for work or school, don't make a big deal of it. If your dog sees that you're relaxed and confident, he will more likely feel that way too.

2 Keep your dog's energy calm. Make sure the dog is calm and relaxed before you leave or enter the home. Take your dog for a long walk or play a vigorous game of fetch in the backyard before you leave in the morning. The exercise will help calm your dog down and help him stay relaxed when you leave.

3) A little company helps. If you must leave your dog for long stretches of time while you work, your dog will benefit from some company during the day. If you're able to come home for lunch, use that time to exercise together. If your schedule doesn't allow that, then hire a professional dog walker to let your dog have some exercise and human contact. The activity will keep your dog calm, and the companionship will keep her happy.

4) Boredom is the enemy. While you're gone, make sure your dog has plenty to keep him entertained. A bored dog can become anxious and destructive, so keep his favorite toys where he can easily find them in your absence. If he's able to play, he'll feel less anxious while you're gone.

TRANSITION:
Your New Relationship

About one year after my divorce, I met a beautiful Dominican woman named Jahira Dar. She was working as a celebrity stylist at Dolce & Gabbana clothing store, where I buy some of my clothes for the TV show. I was taking the elevator up to the men's department when it stopped on the women's floor. The elevator doors opened up, and I saw her. So even though the elevator stopped in the women's department, I stepped out and introduced myself to Jahira. After a brief conversation, I asked her to dinner. A few days later, I began sending her photos of Junior and Coco, our family's Chihuahua.

After several months of dating, I decided it was time to introduce Jahira to the pack. It takes a very special woman to remain

After a smooth introduction, Jahira and Junior are members of the same pack.

calm and assertive when she meets my pack. I introduced her to Junior first. Jahira recalls the meeting: "I was a little nervous because I thought if Junior doesn't like me, then my relationship with Cesar would come to a quick end. But Junior came up to me very deliberately, and he was wagging his tail. Then he sniffed me and lay down next to my feet. Once Junior accepted me, the rest of the pack followed his lead. I was relieved."

The start of a new romantic relationship is an exciting time for any person. To make sure that your dog accepts a new partner, you've got to have a plan. Here are some simple rules to follow when it's time to introduce a new friend to your pack:

1 Go slow. Don't hide your new relationship from your dog, but don't force your dog into a new relationship either. From the beginning, practice "No Touch, No Talk, No Eye

Contact" until the dog gains familiarity with your new relationship and exhibits a calm, submissive state around your new partner.

2 Work together. After compatibility has been established, begin to share duties like feeding and taking the dog for walks. Start by doing these things together and gradually transition some of these responsibilities over to the new member. Be careful not to make your new partner the "outsider" in the household. Establish Rules, Boundaries, and Limitations on how your dog participates in your new relationship. Be consistent in rule setting.

3 Keep it positive. If your dog and your new partner are having a bumpy start to their new relationship, don't fight over the dog, especially not in front of the dog. Even though your dog doesn't understand language, he may associate the new member of your household with negative energy and fighting.

TRANSITION:
A New Baby

Because our dogs are very in tune with us, they know that something is unusual when a baby is on the way. Parents-to-be are typically in an anxious state, and their dogs will pick up on that. Many prospective parents worry about how their dog will adjust to the presence of a new baby. And they should. I've worked with so many dogs whose families didn't handle the transition well. My biggest piece of advice is to make a plan and follow these tips for a smooth transition for preparing your dog and everyone else for the new arrival:

1. Focus on leadership. Nine months is more than enough time to work through most issues and establish the Rules, Boundaries, and Limitations of a new baby, so use this time to shore up your position as Pack Leader and make sure your dog is regularly in a calm, submissive state.

2. Be aware of your energy. A pregnancy affects the entire household. You may feel excited, anxious, or worried—or some combination of all three. Remember, your dog will mirror your emotions.

3. Claim your baby's scent. Before you bring the baby home, introduce an item that contains your baby's scent—such as a blanket—into the home. During this exercise, it's crucial that you set clear boundaries. Challenge the dog to sniff from a distance, while you hold the item. By doing this, you are communicating to your dog that the item is yours; then give the dog permission to sniff the item. You are showing the dog that this new item belongs to you and that the dog will need to follow your rules when around it. This begins the process of creating respect for the baby.

4. Establish boundaries around the nursery. I recommend starting by having the nursery off-limits. Condition your dog to understand that there is an invisible barrier that she may not cross without your permission. Because your dog will have become acclimated to the

Calm, assertive energy is key when introducing a new baby to the family dog.

baby's scent, she will be less likely to violate that rule. Eventually you can allow your dog to explore and sniff certain things in the room with your supervision. Repeat this activity a few times before the baby arrives.

5. Control the introduction of the baby. Before your dog meets the baby, take the dog on a long walk to drain all her energy. Upon returning to the house, don't let the dog in until she is in a calm, submissive state. The person holding the baby must be in a completely calm, assertive state. The dog should be allowed to sniff the baby but must be respectful of distances. During this first meeting, do not bring the baby too close. Eventually, the dog can be allowed to get closer and closer to the baby, provided she remains in a calm, submissive state. If the dog shows any agitation, then end the introduction. Try again later when the dog has calmed down.

6 Don't forget about the dog. A new baby can overwhelm a household, so it's important to take time to pay attention to your dog. A dog does not need toys or special attention to feel wanted; you simply need to try to maintain the routine of daily walks and feeding. This will help your dog feel secure and allow her to relax about the new addition to the family and all the attention the new baby is receiving.

TRANSITION:
Back to School

Every September, when my two sons, Andre and Calvin, head back to school, our whole schedule changes. It takes a few weeks to readjust to the demands of getting up earlier in the mornings, to the stress of being on time for school, and to the after-school routine of sports, homework, and play. After the freedom of summer vacation, Andre and Calvin have to return to the everyday rules, boundaries, and limitations that school naturally gives them. But they're not the only ones.

Although going back to school is usually an exciting, fun time for the humans in the home, it can mean loneliness and boredom for your dog. All summer long, someone is most likely home with your dog. Now that everyone is back to their fall schedules, your dog may feel neglected and can even fall into depression or develop separation anxiety.

Symptoms of depression to watch for include listlessness, lack of energy, loss of appetite, hiding or cowering, and not wanting to play. Unlike depression, separation anxiety (see Chapter 5, page 130) manifests itself in erratic behavior, including excessive barking and whining, frantic clawing at doors, windows, or fences to get out, destructive chewing, and going to the bathroom in the house. Dogs with separation anxiety will be ecstatic when family members return home, while a dog with depression may not even get up from his bed.

If your dog has trouble during back-to-school time, here are some tips for making this transition smoother:

1. Make your dog part of the morning routine. A simple routine can help alleviate the stress your dog feels. Create a schedule with your family that involves everyone. Each morning, someone should get up a little bit early, even just 15 minutes, to take the dog out for a walk or a romp in the backyard before the day starts. Not only will this let your dog know you still care, but releasing that extra energy will make her less likely to be destructive while you are gone.

2. Practice "leaving the house." In the first transition in this chapter, we offered steps for how to make leaving the house stress-free for your dog. Your kids may feel sorry that they're leaving their dog for the day, but they need to refrain from being emotional when they leave. If the dog senses that they're upset, then he will be more likely to be upset too. When everyone comes home from school and work, again, don't make a big deal of it.

3. Have an evening routine. At the end of a long day, it's easy to forget the dog. There's dinner to cook, homework to do, and everyone is tired from the day's activities. But your dog has been waiting for you all day and most likely has unspent

energy. After her dinner, be sure to take her out for some exercise and playtime.

TRANSITION: **Separation and Divorce**

Breakups inevitably come with the dividing up of material assets like a house, cars, and furniture. Any divorce lawyer or marriage therapist will tell you these things are usually the easiest to deal with in a breakup. However, children and pets are not. Unfortunately, custody fights occur all too often. After my former wife, Ilusion, and I divorced, our two sons chose to live with different parents—Andre chose to live with his mother, while Calvin chose to live with me. These kinds of changes are difficult for any family, and they can be very difficult on your dog, who will sense your tension and unease.

If you and your partner are splitting up, here are some strategies to help keep the transition smooth for your dog:

1. Avoid custody fights. The divorce laws of most states treat dogs as property. This means that they can be divided up like cars or furniture. Don't leave it to the court to decide who gets the dogs. Try to work it out with your ex-spouse before the dogs become a casualty of the fight. If you have children from the marriage and these children are close to the dog, I often recommend that the dogs stay with the children. Many people have even begun to include dog ownership in their marriage agreements to avoid a fight in the event of a breakup.

2 Think about the children. Research has shown that children in families with dogs experience less stress after a divorce than those in families without a dog. It stands to reason that dogs as living companions are indispensable in times of transitions and change, and children seem to benefit most by their continued presence in the home.

3 Watch for behavior problems. Dogs who experience a divorce often show aggression when they never had before. The tense energy in a household of divorce can affect dogs in the same way that it does family members. It's important that dogs get lots of exercise during the breakup so they can relieve anxiety and have a break from the stressful environment.

4 Your circumstances will be different. Be honest with yourself about your life choices and how your life will change after divorce. All too often, I see dogs from divorced families brought into the shelters. Spouses who wanted the dog during the divorce discover that they cannot handle the dog postdivorce because they have to work full-time, or they meet another person who doesn't like the dog.

5 Try to stay calm. The most important thing to remember about your dog during a breakup is that your emotions will be mirrored in your dog's behavior. Learning how to calm yourself and project a relaxed and assertive energy around your dog will not only be a good thing for your dog's benefit, but it can also help the rest of the family.

Transition:
Moving and Travel

On average, Americans move every five years. That means that within an average dog's life, you may move two or three times. Psychologists say that moving is on the list of the ten most traumatic events in your life. If that's so, you can imagine the effect moving may have on your dog. Here are some commonsense tips to help ease the transition to a new home, particularly if the move requires long-distance travel:

1 Get a checkup. Consult with a local veterinarian to find out if your dog can handle the trip and what medical precautions may be needed to ensure your dog makes it safely. Generally, dogs can last more than 72 hours without food. Junior and I have traveled all over the world, and I don't feed him on the mornings that we're traveling.

2 Practice. Practice. Practice. Think of your dogs as astronauts. Before they blast off, astronauts practice spending time in a confined space with limited food options. They get used to controlling their anxiety of being behind walls for such a long period of time in space. Do the same for your dog using a crate or carrier, preferably the same kennel or carrier that the dog will travel in when it's time for the journey. Gradually increase the time she spends in it.

3 Make the crate a great place to be. Help your dog associate the travel crate with positive things. Don't feel sorry for her or get upset. She will immediately sense your emotions and this could cause anxiety.

4 Do your homework. If you're moving to a foreign country, be sure to research the regulations about quarantine. In some countries, certain breeds are outlawed, and you don't want your dog confiscated at customs. If your dog is put into quarantine, try to visit her every day if you can. Ask the animal control authorities for permission to take her for walks.

5 Get a room! If you are making the journey by car, be sure to research pet-friendly hotels along your route. Do not leave the dog in the car alone overnight. If your dog howls or barks in your hotel room, he is probably nervous and just trying to communicate. Do not reward the behavior by giving him affection or sympathy. Try taking your dog out for a long walk to drain his energy.

6 Exercise before you hit the road. No matter how you are traveling with your dog, make sure to take your dog for an extra long run or walk on the morning of the trip to deplete her energy. The journey will be less stressful to her if she has low energy levels.

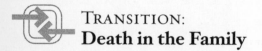

TRANSITION:
Death in the Family

The story of a German shepherd named Capitán captivated

the nation back in 2011. Capitán ran away from home after his owner, Manuel Guzman, died in 2006. A week later, Guzman's family, who live in Córdoba, Argentina, found the heartbroken dog grieving at the graveside. The dog spent the next six years in the cemetery and was taken care of by cemetery workers who fed and looked after the dog.

A dog that has lost a companion or member of the pack may show signs of distress, including a lack of appetite, aloof behavior, and even a demand for attention and affection. Confidence and a feeling of belonging to a pack disappear with the loss of a pack member. Some dogs may wander around the house, trying to reconcile the lingering scent of deceased pack members with the fact that they cannot be found anymore.

Here are some tips for helping dogs move through the grieving process:

1. Dogs do mourn. Expect your dog to exhibit some symptoms of grief, like loss of appetite and sluggishness. This is natural.

2. Dogs know the scent of death. If possible, let the dog smell something from the body so that the dog has closure.

3. Keep up your routine. Don't suddenly become inactive with the dog. This is the time when the dog needs long walks the most. Try changing the walk path to change her state of mind, or take the dog to a new place to walk. Don't feel sorry for the dog, but try to maintain as consistent a routine as possible. Continue to show strong leadership.

4. Life goes on. Give the dog new challenges, new environments, and new adventures as soon as possible so he recognizes that life is moving on.

For as long as I can remember, dogs have been my best teachers, and my first right-hand dog, Daddy, taught me one of the most important, and one of the most difficult, lessons at the end of his life. I was lucky enough to work with Daddy for 16 years, and he taught me what mastering acceptance looks like. Everywhere we went together, he spread peace. Cats, rabbits, people who disliked pit bulls — Daddy accepted them all.

Near the end of Daddy's life in February 2010, we had an incredible moment of eye contact between us. He gazed at me with his honey-colored eyes in a way that went straight to my heart and shook me to the core. Looking back now, I think it was Daddy's way of telling me I had become too comfortable with my life, in my business and in my relationships. His death, a few days later, was part of an emotional wake-up call. It was Daddy's way of telling me, "Your whole life needs to change."

Daddy's passing was difficult for me and my entire family. We mourned his death and tried to celebrate his life achievements. About two months later, my proud blue pit bull Junior took over as my right hand. This transition took place very naturally. One day, Junior and I walked together to the top of my mountain at the DPC and he gave me a look that reminded me of the look Daddy had given me many times before. This was a look of boundless love and support, as if Junior was saying, "It's going to be OK, Cesar. I'm here for you, but you need to be here for me, too."

Being a Pack Leader is not only about guiding your pack through transitions, it's also about getting yourself through

Daddy and I shared 16 amazing years together.

them, too. No member of the pack—including its leader—can get stuck in the past or become anxious about the future when faced with change.

Change and transitions are nature's way of testing pack leaders and further developing their leadership skills. It is during difficult times of change where leadership is most needed. In my travels over the past few years, I've met so many people who are struggling in the face of very serious life transitions brought on by all kinds of events—from economic hardship to fallout from natural disasters. But the thing that unites them all is that these trials are the kinds of thing that can bring out the best in us and our dogs. And if we are tuned in to nature and respecting the Core Principles, we can use this knowledge to make us stronger and confidently move forward.

CHAPTER EIGHT

The Fulfillment Formula

For several summers, I spoke at an annual event in Aspen, Colorado, called "Cesar Whispers in Aspen," presented by Friends of the Aspen Animal Shelter. It's a big social event attended by dog lovers and many of the city's affluent part-time residents who make Aspen their summer hideout. There are often heads of Fortune 500 companies, entertainers, media figures, and politicians in the audience.

Amazingly, I am invited to speak about dogs and what I call "pack leadership." What could I, a poor working-class kid from Mexico, possibly have to offer some of the most accomplished people in the United States? It turns out, I have a lot to offer. I know that the secret to improving their relationships with their dogs can also change their own lives for the better. The secret? I call it the fulfillment formula.

This formula, developed over many years of working with dogs and humans, is the best way I know to access the power of leadership. By engaging in a regular program of Exercise, Discipline, and Affection (in that order), you are better equipped to handle anything that comes your way in life (see Chapter 4, page 81). This formula is grounded in the Natural Dog Laws and the Core Principles we covered earlier in the book. The formula sharpens your instincts and is key to developing calm, assertive energy, which will help you feel more fulfilled in everything you do. Practice this formula, and you'll have a better relationship with your dog, your loved ones, and yourself.

The fulfillment formula is simple, but following it consistently isn't always so easy. If it were, then everyone could do it, and I would be out of a job. Dogs would be balanced, and everyone would be happy. But what makes it challenging is that it takes time. It takes commitment. It takes dedication. It takes the ability to stick to it, even when it's difficult. And it requires the ability to assess your life honestly and recognize when things are out of balance.

To help you understand the power of the fulfillment formula, I am going to break down each component to ensure you know how to apply it to enrich your dog's and your own life.

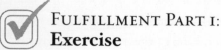

FULFILLMENT PART 1:
Exercise

The first step for creating a balanced dog pack is also rule number one in the fulfillment formula—exercise. Any time I've struggled in my life, exercise brought me back. Now it gives me purpose, energy, focus, consistency, and an outlet for releasing tension, stress, and excess energy.

For humans, exercise can take on an element of spirituality—it uplifts you, transforms you, releases you from whatever

In-line skating with your dog is a great way to exhaust pent-up energy.

burdens you. When I began the course to correct my life after divorce, I started waking up at 4:30 in the morning with renewed energy. I would either run with the dogs or get into the boxing ring with a trainer named Terry Norris, who once knocked out Sugar Ray Leonard.

Everyone knows exercise is good for you, even though 25 percent of Americans don't do it on a regular basis. Even fewer people engage in the type of vigorous regular exercise I believe is essential, both for you and your dog. You sleep better, look better, think clearer, and live longer. Sitting for prolonged periods of time can undo the good effects even a regular program of vigorous exercise delivers. One study, published last year in the journal *Circulation,* concluded that for each hour of television a person watches a day, the risk of dying from heart-related problems rises by 11 percent.

BE ACTIVE IN THE MOMENT

The best way to stay off of your couch is to get a dog. During a visit to Canada, I met a young man who was working as a clerk in a Canadian Tire store. Severely overweight, he decided to start exercising with his dog after watching my TV show. This once obese young man lost more than a hundred pounds and started his own morning dog-walking business. He looks great, feels great, and is healthy again.

When I walk my pack in the hills surrounding the DPC, the feeling of being in the moment is incredibly strong. I am connected to Mother Nature and doing something good for my body. Someone asked me recently what I think about when I am walking 50 dogs. The answer is *nothing*. For me, walking dogs is about feeling, not thinking . . . It's about feeling calmness and peace.

To many people, the dog walk is a stressful experience. We're worried about an approaching dog or about a neighbor we know doesn't like dogs. We're worried about our dog barking, running too fast, or pulling on the lead. This is not being in the moment, and you will never achieve calmness in this state of mind. It's no wonder that dogs in the United States get the least exercise of dogs anywhere. Owners are too stressed out.

Try staying in the moment on your next dog walk. Try not to think about the day at the office or the kids at school. Try especially not to worry about how your dog might act up or misbehave on the walk. Instead, visualize a calm, successful, and enjoyable time together. Stay focused on the sights, smells, and sounds of the walk itself. Concentrate on the unspoken cues between you and your dog. If your mind starts to wander or you feel yourself becoming anxious, bring your attention to your breath. You can also use the energy exercises you learned in Chapter 4.

THE RIGHT AMOUNT OF EXERCISE

The amount of exercise your dog requires will, of course, depend upon your dog's energy level, physical abilities, and, in some cases, breed characteristics. Senior or low-energy dogs may wear themselves out after a trip or two around the block, while high-energy dogs, particularly from the working, sporting, and hound groups, may require over an hour of walking, and you may need to add some jogging, running, or hiking. Although puppies can be very energetic, they also lack the muscle tone for very strenuous exercise, but they will generally let you know when they've had enough by going into rest mode when their energy is drained.

In all cases, remember the following points when exercising with your dog:

1. Watch out for overheating. This goes for you and your dog; if you feel too hot, then your dog probably does, too. Use caution on very hot days, trying to exercise early in the morning or in the evening, and bring along plenty of water. If your dog begins to show signs of heatstroke, seek medical attention immediately. Symptoms of heatstroke include heavy panting and labored breathing; excess salivation; dry, pale gums; weakness or confusion; vomiting; and diarrhea. If you cannot get your dog to the veterinarian immediately, then pour cool or tepid (never ice-cold) water on her body. If possible, also use a fan blowing cool air in conjunction with the water.

2. Be consistent with your exercise schedule. Running two miles on a weekend and then doing nothing during the week can cause extra stress on your dog's joints and yours.

It is better to take multiple shorter walks throughout the week—at least twice a day—than to try to cram all of the exercise into one session. If you absolutely cannot get out every day of the week to walk your dog, then find indoor alternatives:

- Have your dog run up and down the stairs (with your supervision, of course).
- Create an obstacle course with household objects to practice agility.
- Hide treats around the house for your dog to hunt and find.
- Play "keep away" or fetch.
- Introduce your dog to a treadmill, and then teach her how to run or trot on it.

Whether you walk two times every day (preferable) or alternate indoor days with walk days, keeping the schedule as regular as possible will help your dog maintain balance.

3 Take care of your dog's feet. Running on cement—especially when hot from the sun—can cause injury to a puppy's footpads, even causing them to slough off. Give a young dog plenty of breaks by walking or running on softer surfaces, like grass, until they have built up the adult calluses that will protect them. For adult dogs, be aware of hot surfaces, particularly asphalt, which can burn them fairly quickly on sunny days, particularly in the mid-afternoon. White or light-colored concrete does not retain heat in the same way and is much safer. In very hot weather, try to spend a minimal amount of time crossing streets or parking lots, and allow your dog regular cool-down time on grass. A good test for places you shouldn't let your dog walk for too long is to go barefoot yourself. If your feet cannot take the heat, your dog probably isn't enjoying it either.

4 Know your dog's and your own limits. If your dog is in a calm, submissive state, then she will let you know when she's had enough exercise. Also, as you spend more time being in the moment on walks, you will become very aware of your dog's state of mind and begin to know when she has had enough. If you're halfway out and either one of you gets too tired to go on, there's nothing wrong with sitting quietly together for a few minutes, until you're ready to resume. Also, knowing your dog's limits will help you to spot any possible medical problems or other causes for concern well ahead of time—for example, a dog that loves to take long runs three times a day but suddenly wants to stop during a short walk may have a condition worthy of a vet visit.

Exercise is important and healthy for you and your dog. When shared properly on walks, it will keep your dog balanced, keep you in shape, and provide you both with the best possible bonding experience.

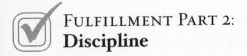

Fulfillment Part 2: **Discipline**

Like *dominance* and *control, discipline* is another one of those words that people can easily perceive as negative, as I discussed

Discipline is an essential part of fulfilling your dog's needs.

in the "How to Read This Book" section (see page 15). But notice that this word is very similar to *disciple,* and they both come from the Latin words that describe a student, as well as the instruction a student receives. So, rather than thinking of discipline as punishment, it is better to think of it as you teaching and your dog learning, working together as a team.

When I first came to the United States, I saw quickly how undisciplined American society can be when it comes to dogs. American dogs get to eat whatever they want, sleep wherever they want, and sit wherever they want. American dogs have several beds, many toys, and lots of treats. In Mexico, dogs don't have any beds, and they get a stick if they want to have fun or play catch. There's nothing wrong with giving a dog toys or beds to sleep in. The problem comes when dogs start being treated like little humans. This is generally the first step in losing control of boundaries with a dog. When you see dogs that continually ignore the direction of their owners, it's usually because they have not been disciplined. But these dogs can be turned around, if their owners set up the proper environment with rules and boundaries.

I went through a similar situation not too long ago when I recognized that things were out of balance in my family life. I had received a heartbreaking call from a psychiatrist, who told me that my son Calvin was being put on medication for ADHD. ADHD, attention deficit/hyperactivity disorder, is a common childhood behavioral disorder that can be difficult to diagnose and even harder to understand.

The divorce wasn't just hard on me; it took a big toll on my children. It divided our family, and it injected a lot of uncertainty into Calvin's life. When I think back, it seems so clear: Calvin's diet had deteriorated to meals consisting of sugary cereal and candy bars. He looked sullen, tired, and unmotivated. He wasn't doing well in school, and he was becoming more disrespectful to adults.

After that phone call, I realized that—more than anything else—Calvin needed discipline and he needed to be understood. The divorce had disrupted all the routines of the house. It had taken away the Pack Leader of the family, and there was a leadership void. It was up to me as his dad to reestablish Rules, Boundaries, and Limitations with him, and practice Exercise, Discipline, and Affection. I could use this structure to create a more stable environment for my son and hopefully help him find his balance again.

A Zen psychologist recently noted that the definition of discipline is "remembering exactly what you want." That's an accurate description of how we addressed this situation with Calvin. I remembered the kind of son I wanted Calvin to be, I recalled the type of parent I could be, and I stepped into this role. I built a stronger support team around Calvin—a new school that would be attentive to his needs; new friends who were focused on sports or hobbies; and Jahira and I, who were equally focused on being caring, patient adults. We all worked together to get Calvin off of medication and back to a healthy life.

Discipline is about having your mind in the right place. This can only be achieved by knowing Rules, Boundaries, and Limitations. Here is a short exercise that Calvin and I used to help bring our minds back to the right place:

1. Think about a time in your life when you felt unstoppable. What was something you wanted without hesitation? A relationship? A job? Acknowledgment from your family? Go back to your childhood if you must, because that is a time when instinct is unobstructed by human forces and time.

2. Write for ten minutes about that unstoppable time in your life. What were you thinking, feeling, or even hoping for or praying about? What did it feel like? Describe your energy, your emotions. What challenges did you overcome to get what you wanted in a hurry?

3. Now write down how your life would be different right now if you approached it in the same manner as you did to get what you wanted back then, knowing you could not fail? How would this affect your relationship with yourself, your work, the people around you, and your dog?

4. What are the three things you could do to trigger this state of mind at any time you wanted? What are the three things

you would like to achieve in an unstoppable way? What are three steps you can take now to start achieving those goals?

This little exercise recenters your mind and channels your energy.

FULFILLMENT PART 3:
Affection

Love is one of the greatest gifts we can share. It's one of the many reasons why I love dogs so much. They are affectionate animals, and they love unconditionally. However, affection that is shared with a dog at the wrong time can be detrimental to her. You cannot love a dog out of chewing on your new shoes, just as you cannot love an alcoholic out of drinking, or love a child into cleaning up his room. Animals and people alike need Rules, Boundaries, and Limitations—even when it comes to love. Dogs

Unconditional love is just one of the many gifts dogs give to us.

don't accept bribes for good behavior, and bribes seldom create lasting results with people either.

Affection comes in many forms, and it isn't always food. A dog that is a family pet may get affection in the form of treats, brushing, or petting. But affection can also be acknowledgment, a favorite toy, or a playdate with another compatible dog.

The important thing to remember is to never give your dog affection when he is not in a calm, submissive state. Never comfort a dog that is anxious, excited, or fearful—this will just confuse the dog. Because dogs live in the moment, your affection will not change their state. It just tells your dog, "It is all right for you to feel this way." Affection at the wrong time will reinforce unwanted behavior because your dog will learn to use that behavior to earn your affection.

With people, affection is a little more complex. As we discussed in Chapter 2 (see page 34), humans are intellectual and emotional (dogs are instinctual), so affection takes on many more forms and meanings for people. Affection can be given at many times and under different emotional states with people. We show affection to reassure each other (hugs), to celebrate (high fives), and to love (kisses). We have so many dimensions and aspects because humans are emotional creatures. But the reward of affection can also help us and our loved ones stick to routines of exercise and discipline. When we are balanced people, it is easier for us to give and receive affection. This last part of the fulfillment formula can be a powerful motivator.

Now that you understand the fulfillment formula, in the next chapter, I will share with you real-life stories of people who have used it in their own lives to solve problems or help other people. Their stories are inspirational to me, and I hope they will be to you as well.

CHAPTER NINE

Enrich Your Dog, Enrich Your Life

My fulfillment formula is the best way I know to harness the power of pack leadership. By engaging in a program of Exercise, Discipline, and Affection, you will be better equipped to handle anything that comes your way in life. The formula sharpens your instincts and is key to developing calm, assertive energy and to feel more fulfilled in everything you do.

Based on the fundamentals and techniques I have developed by working with dogs and their human companions, this formula can make human lives better. It literally saved mine. It helped me repair my family relationships and restore my business and my own sense of self.

A REAL LIFESAVER:
Captain Angus Alexander

Along the way, I have met many people who have applied the fulfillment formula to their lives with great success. The head

Lifeguard Angus Alexander and his dog Jack are on patrol.

of the L.A. County Lifeguard program adopted elements of the formula into his instruction for teaching junior lifeguards.

"Many of the things we do around here we do because of Cesar," says Captain Angus Alexander. He runs his program from the Los Angeles County Fire Department Lifeguard Headquarters on the beach next to the Santa Monica Pier. Years ago, this spot was home to the original Muscle Beach outdoor fitness center. Today, it's a mix of tourists and locals looking for fun in the California sun.

As duty officer for the entire county coastline—all 72 miles of it—Captain Alexander, 50 years old but ruddy and robust as a teenager, coordinates ocean search and rescue efforts and makes sure the U.S. Coast Guard, L.A. County Sheriff's Department, and his 600 beach lifeguards are working in harmony to keep tens of thousands of beachgoers safe. His secret? "Exercise, Discipline, and Affection, in that order," he says. "I also enforce Rules, Boundaries, and Limitations."

Captain Alexander is a longtime fan of my TV show. After training his own black Lab Jack to save swimmers using my techniques (Jack stars in "Dog rescues man from the ocean" on YouTube), he decided to apply the principles to his staff. Early morning calisthenics (exercise) are followed by mandatory sweeping, cleaning, waxing, and maintenance (discipline), a routine that's rewarded with regular earned perks (affection—in this case, food). "My wife is a gourmet chef," Captain Alexander says. "My lifeguards know if they stay fit and do their job, I'll take care of them with the best pasta dinner you can possibly imagine."

The results are remarkable. His lifeguards log close to 10,000 surf rescues a year. Drownings are down by 50 percent from ten years ago (in 2011, there was only one), and Captain Alexander's team has never been more cohesive or focused, he says.

HEALTHY DOG, HEALTHY HUMAN: Jillian Michaels

When I teach people the fulfillment formula, the goal is a healthy, well-adjusted dog. It also turns out that getting owners to step into their role as a Pack Leader is just as good for them as it is for their dogs. Everything starts with the first step in my fulfillment formula—exercise.

Jillian Michaels knows a thing or two about exercise. And now, after working with me, she also knows about the fulfillment formula. Jillian is a no-nonsense health and wellness expert, known for her work as a fitness trainer, life coach, author, and star of the hit TV show *The Biggest Loser.* She also happens to be crazy about dogs, a love that started when she was an overweight young girl. "I was

Jillian Michaels and I talk about her dogs.

very lonely, and all I had were dogs—they were like siblings to me. In my darkest, loneliest times, my dogs have been there for me."

These days, Jillian has her own battle with weight firmly under control, and she inspires countless people to change their lives for the better. She's also the owner of three rescue dogs: Seven, an Italian greyhound mix; Harley, a terrier mix; and Richard, a Chihuahua. Jillian may be an expert in exercise, but when she needed help with Seven, she knew she had to turn to another expert. She came to me. The problem with Seven was that she would snarl at Jillian's horse and run under his legs, and Jillian was afraid the dog would injure herself—or the horse.

I worked with Seven, but I also spent some time with Jillian, trainer to trainer. By teaching Jillian how to use the fulfillment formula, she was able to completely correct Seven's bad behavior. In Jillian's own words, "I know it seems like magic, but it's not. I was able to implement that new attitude into different parts of her day. She's had a giant change in personality."

The second step in my fulfillment formula is discipline, which is also a very important part of Jillian's work with people who have eating disorders and weight issues. She advises them on the importance of a daily routine, and once again, the fulfillment formula and dogs come into the picture: "On those days when you don't feel like getting off the couch, your dog will nudge, pull, and whine until he gets his daily exercise. Instead of viewing this behavior as annoying, you can see it as motivating."

After her work with me, Jillian was able to take what she learned about the fulfillment formula and apply a new way of thinking to her work with her clients. "I spend a lot of time trying to figure out why people behave the way they do, and now when I'm having a hard time, sometimes I'll just go for the change and work on the deeper stuff simultaneously. Change the behavior, then explore what's underneath."

Jillian may forgo affection at times and sometimes even chooses a direct and harsh path. While she strongly believes the best way to help people is often through brutal honesty, she does and can provide affectionate support at the right time. "I think a dog is the purest form of energy you can tap into, that unconditional love. It doesn't matter if you think you're ugly or people won't love you, or you lost your job—you know the dog's going to love you."

TURNING MY LIFE AROUND:
Cesar Millan

For Captain Alexander and Jillian, the fulfillment formula improved their lives. But in my case, the formula saved my life. It's as simple as that.

I've met many incredible people who share their stories of how they've applied some of my fundamentals to improve their own lives, but none touched my heart more than a person I met at a book signing in November 2011. His name was Mike. And I will never forget him.

My manager and I were in Toronto, Canada, to do some retail store appearances. I was signing autographs, shaking hands, and taking photos. It was toward the end of a long day when a young man, around 30 years old, shuffled up to me. He was thin and pale. My manager tried to move in between us, but the young man was persistent and came within inches of my face.

"Cesar," he said, "my name is Mike, and I have AIDS. I came here today to tell you that you saved my life." I froze for a split second, and then I grabbed this young man and gave him the biggest hug I've ever given anyone in my life.

Mike went on to explain that he had given up all hope of living after he was hospitalized with AIDS. While in the hospital, he discovered the *Dog Whisperer* TV show. Because they air multiple episodes a day in Canada, Mike was quickly hooked on the show and took it to heart.

Soon, he began applying the foundations of pack leadership, including the Exercise, Discipline, and Affection formula, in his own life. Slowly, he found his purpose again. He accepted his medical condition. With the determination of a pit bull, he decided he was going to move on and begin living again.

Mike had become stuck and could not move forward. That changed when he introduced the Exercise, Discipline, and Affection approach to his daily routine. That combination allowed him to muster up the will to live and beat his disease. Of all the things I thought I might accomplish, I never thought

I would help save someone else's life. Mike's story was a gift, one that helped me realize just how blessed I have been.

During the taxi ride back to the Toronto airport, I was reflecting on Mike's story—the journey he had taken, and the fact that I was able to affect it—and I found it such an emotional moment that I began to cry. I then realized how much my own life had changed over the previous year, beginning when my former wife, Ilusion, told me that she wanted a divorce. Since that moment, my journey had been a harrowing one, filled with tremendous pain and uncertainty. On that cab ride, I saw just how fortunate I was to be able to help someone like Mike. It hit me that I had emerged from that dark time a stronger, wiser man, more grateful for life's good fortune and more determined than ever to be a strong Pack Leader.

I had already been in pain when I received the divorce news in March 2010. My beloved pit bull Daddy had died just a month earlier. Daddy's death had deeply shaken me, but I knew my grief would pass. In March, I was in Ireland as part of a whirlwind European tour in which I was speaking to crowds of over 7,000 people. On the morning of the Dublin presentation, I received a transatlantic phone call from my wife in Los Angeles, saying that she wanted a divorce. I had assumed things were going great. But little did I know or understand what was about to hit me. My life was going to change forever, and I—Cesar Millan, the Pack Leader to millions of dog owners all over the world—could neither control nor change its direction. It was terrifying.

Over the years, Ilusion and I struggled to balance our innate differences with the demands of marriage, a TV show, and two children. It wasn't easy. We had broken up and gotten back together several times. After 20 years together, and with so much life ahead, the ending came abruptly. I wasn't ready.

Because of the divorce, I was forced to see things as they really were for the very first time. As I examined the business decisions I'd agreed to over the years, I was confronted by how poor many of them were. I had given up my rights and my name. I had entered into contracts I never should have signed. My partners were saying one thing, but their contracts read very differently. I realized I didn't even own the name "Dog Whisperer."

At the end of the day, I owned only my clothes, my car, and the Dog Psychology Center. Everything else—including the TV show and the house in which I had lived and raised a family—belonged to other people. As my business manager reviewed my financial status, he informed me that I was broke. I actually had a negative net worth after seven years of being on TV, and I didn't know why.

At first I was angry, and I retreated to the Dog Psychology Center, where I withdrew from people entirely. I wanted no human contact. Full of negative energy, I would brood and sit for hours with my pack. Eventually, the stress and sadness I was experiencing took its toll on my dogs. The pack's size shrunk from 20 dogs before Daddy's passing to just a handful. Instinctually, the pack knew its leader was unstable, and they sought and found other homes. I was devastated that I couldn't help myself and I couldn't help my own pack.

I've seen dogs react like this to stress. When a dog is out of equilibrium, he quickly goes into a negative or panicked state. He doesn't want to be with other dogs or with humans. Isolation is a tangible reaction to an unstable environment, which is the root of virtually every canine behavior problem: biting, chewing, digging, excessive barking, territoriality, and aggression. Those issues are easy enough to fix in dogs. To fix them in myself, it was 10,000 times harder.

An animal-like rage ran through me: I wanted to destroy things; I wanted to destroy my business; I wanted to hurt myself and the people around me. I had never felt so emotionally devastated. I could not forgive myself for what was happening. I was overcome by a sense of failure, and I lost all confidence in myself.

Few people knew what was really going on inside of me, except for my brother, Erick, and my manager. I hid it from my sons, my business associates, and even my parents. Like Mike from Toronto, I wondered if I had a reason to live.

The lowest point came in May 2010, when I stopped eating. I was shocked to see I dropped to 135 pounds from 175 in just 40 days. I stopped working, and I rarely slept more than four hours a day. During this time, Ilusion and I were separated but not legally divorced, and I went over to the house to try to reconcile our marriage. Our conversation went poorly, and at the end of it, I knew our marriage was over.

I also thought my life was over, so I did a stupid thing. I tried to end my life by taking some pills. I don't know what I took or how many. I just remember the feeling of how badly I wanted to be someplace else, anywhere but where I was. The next thing I remember, I was being rushed to the hospital in an ambulance. I demanded that the ambulance driver take me to my grandfather's farm in Mexico. I wanted to be away from it all.

The next day, I was checked into a psychiatric hospital for observation. Three days later, I was released, and like Mike, I was determined to reestablish my inner balance and find a new purpose for my life. I would find that new purpose only after I embraced my own fundamentals and the fulfillment formula again.

I couldn't fight the direction my life had taken. I had to accept it. Once I did, everything looked brighter. The energy came

Seeing all the people at the 2012 National Pack Walk reminds me of what an amazing privilege it is to be Pack Leader.

back. I started eating and sleeping again. Slowly, I was moving forward, thanks in part to the super pack of people around me and the dogs who remained at the Dog Psychology Center. I brought regular exercise back into my life. I created a set of Rules, Boundaries, and Limitations for myself to follow. And lastly, I shared affection with the friends, family, and dogs who gave me the motivation and inspiration to get back up again.

People often wonder how I get such quick results with the dogs I rehabilitate. As I've said before, the answer is simple: Dogs live in the moment. They aren't consumed by mistakes from the past or fear of the future. As I began to stop looking backward and to stop dreading the future, I started to regain my appreciation for what was happening in the here and now.

Now I have rebuilt my pack—I currently have 22 dogs; I have just finished shooting a new TV show, *Cesar Millan's Leader of the Pack;* my son Calvin is living with me and starting a TV career of his own; and I have a beautiful girlfriend named Jahira who cares about me and cares about the pack like it's her own.

I have turned my life around, thanks to all the experiences I shared with dogs over the past 22 years of my life. Without the lessons they've taught me and the wisdom I've gained from working with them, I might not have been able to start all over again.

What I realized is that being a Pack Leader is not just about a moment in time. A leader must continue to evolve, learn, and encounter life's challenges head-on. A leader is not afraid or ashamed to lean on his pack and allow the other pack members to help maintain balance. And no matter how difficult the obstacle, don't let yourself get stuck.

These challenges allowed me to find strength in myself and carry on through my own darkest times. And whenever I find myself exhausted or asking whether I am following the right path, I think back to that moment in Toronto in 2011. I think back to Mike and the fulfillment formula that may have helped in some small way to save his life. Mike helped provide me with strength in my darkest times as well, and he reminded me of the incredible things people—and their dogs—can achieve with the right formula. Wherever you are, Mike . . . God bless.

Additional Resources

DOG TRAINING AND BEHAVIOR
Cesar's Way *www.cesarsway.com*
Cesar Millan's online home

International Association of Canine Professionals
canineprofessionals.com
Searchable database to find a professional dog trainer in your area

BREED RESEARCH
American Kennel Club *www.akc.org*
Comprehensive place to learn about dog breeds and breeders

FINDING A PET
Best Friends Animal Society *www.bestfriends.org*
Animal sanctuary and nationwide network of shelters and
rescue groups

North Shore Animal League *www.animalleague.org*
World's largest no-kill animal rescue and adoption agency

Petfinder *www.petfinder.com*
Lists hundreds of thousands of adoptable animals from across
the United States

YOUR DOG'S HEALTH
American Veterinary Medical Association *www.avma.org*
Information about dog behavior, health, and product recalls

MyVeterinarian.com *www.myveterinarian.com*
Searchable nationwide database of veterinarians

Spay USA *spayusa.org*
Nationwide network of spay and neuter resources

ANIMAL WELFARE RESOURCES
American Society for the Prevention of Cruelty to Animals
www.aspca.org

The Humane Society of the United States *humanesociety.org*

Last Chance for Animals *www.lcanimal.org*

TRAVELING WITH YOUR DOG
PetFriendlyTravel.com *www.petfriendlytravel.com*
Travel information on pet-friendly destinations

Dog Vacay *dogvacay.com*
Find low-cost in-home boarding and dog professionals in your
area

ACTIVITIES FOR YOUR DOG
K9 Nose Work *www.k9nosework.com*
Introduction to the dog sport of tracking and scenting

North American Flyball Association *www.flyball.org*
Information about flyball training and tournaments

United States Dog Agility Association *www.usdaa.com*
Information about dog agility competitions and classes

Illustrations Credits